Standards in the Classroom

Sara Davis Powell, Ph.D.

Teacher Created Materials, Inc.

Cover Series Design by Darlene Spivak

Made in U.S.A.

ISBN 1-57690-482-2

Order Number TCM 2482

www.teachercreated.com

Table of Contents

Introduction

The concept of standards is not new. Standards express clear expectations. They describe what is to be achieved. Organizations set standards, the public demands standards, and the government mandates standards. Children's pajamas must meet stringent fire-retardant standards, and their car seats must adhere to safety standards. The Environmental Protection Agency regulates contaminant levels in schools, and pediatricians must be licensed. School lunches, bus transportation, disease immunizations, and teacher certification all operate in an environment where standards ensure consistent quality. The list goes on. As a nation, we promote child welfare through the use of standards.

Now standards have moved into the world of academics. Most would agree that we have always had standards, more or less organized, explicit or implicit, to guide us in schools. "Less organized" and "implicit" were the closest description to reality until the 1990s. Prior to the '90s, some local districts and some states set standards through their prescribed curriculum. Then, in 1989, the National Council of Teachers of Mathematics (NCTM) responded to the bleak picture painted in the 1983 *A Nation at Risk* report by establishing standards arrived at through consensus of America's math educators. Also, in the fall of 1989, President Bush and the governors of all 50 states agreed on the need for, and then wrote *Goals 2000*. In his 1990 State of the Union address, President Bush declared that education was a priority on the national agenda. Standards in academics were catapulted to the foreground of interest and priority.

The controversial nature of the standards debate; the rapid, premature formation of strong opinions by both politicians and educators on either side of the issue; and the potential for long term gains in future generations of students all demand that every individual involved in this issue have some familiarity with the historical context in which the current standards movement exists. Readers are encouraged to freshen their historical perspective on this issue by reviewing Chapter 2, rather than head directly into the nuts and bolts chapters.

In the United States, the responsibility for education rests with the states, almost all of which have responded to national organizations like NCTM and Goals 2000 by writing state standards. For educators, the standards serve as powerful organizers that will help affect systemic reform. The hope is that academic standards will align education components such as curriculum, instruction, materials, and teacher professional development to ultimately benefit the students in schools across each state and throughout the nation. National organizations have adopted standards for their particular disciplines, but the concept of national standards, either voluntary or mandated, is an issue over which the debate still rages. For now, at least, we rely on state standards to "realize the dream of learning for all" (Schmoker and Marzano, 1999, p. 19).

Just the Facts . . . The 5 W's and the H of Standards

Newspaper journalists know that there are essential components to reporting a story—give the facts, inform the reader, set the stage. This means the five W's and the H: who, what, where, when, why, and how. The standards "story" is front page news in education!

Who?

Who makes decisions concerning standards? Agatha Christie would be proud to have conjured up this cast of characters. Since the standards movement has widespread political and educational implications, both politicians and educators at the local, state and national levels have very defined roles. Policy decisions commonly rest with school, district and state organizations, yet national educational subject area organizations and professional educational bodies have developed vital content and watchdog roles. At the user level, teachers and students ultimately determine the effectiveness of the product produced.

> . . . both politicians and educators at the local, state and national levels have very defined roles.

The decision on what will be contained in standards documents rests at the defining level of the organization. Committees made up of representatives within subject organizations wrestle with content and skills to decide what to include in the standards sanctioned by these governing bodies. States set standards across grade levels and subject areas. To whom are we referring when we say "state"? In most cases, personnel of state departments of education, assisted by committees of educators, spend many hours examining subject area organizations' (National Council of Teachers of English, etc.) sets of standards along with established state curricula. Together they decide on what is important in each subject area and at each grade level in terms of what students should know and be able to do.

The decision concerning assessment of standards at the state level again rests with state departments of education in concert with committees of educators. These assessments are piloted in schools so that the "who" of testing standards is expanded to students and their teachers.

Who implements standards? Classroom teachers are responsible for making standards a reality in the academic lives of their students. Building-level and district-level administrators have the responsibility of supporting teachers who willingly guide their curriculum and instruction by published standards, as well as prompting those who have not yet embraced the standards.

Who has a stake in accountability issues surrounding state standards? Any and all of us fall into this category. From students to teachers to administrators to state department personnel to legislators, along with parents and community members—we all are affected by the mastery, or the lack thereof, of standards.

> **Who has a stake in accountability issues surrounding state standards? Any and all of us fall into this category.**

What?

This book will concentrate on state standards. There are no established, generally accepted national standards. Attempts to establish them are politically charged. Because education is constitutionally a state responsibility and most school systems answer to local boards of elected citizens, the chances that we will arrive at a common core of valued knowledge that teachers should teach and students should learn are slim. For now, we have state standards. Most states have specialized assessments for addressing standards. As the new millennium begins, 49 of our 50 states have standards; 80% of these states report they impose sanctions when school results are low; and 55% of the states report that they have assessments tightly aligned to their standards (McREL, 1999).

A standard is a description of what is to be achieved, an example to be aimed for. There is a difference between a standard and standardization. Standardization simply implies "sameness." A standard is much more. It is a level to which to aspire.

Different books and organizations preface the word "standards" with different descriptors. Perhaps the two most widely used descriptors, and the ones used in this book, are content and performance. Content standards go beyond content knowledge to include skills, so content standards encompass what we want students to both know and be able to do. Performance standards refer to the assessment we impose to measure if the standards have been met.

Where?

The standards-based education movements is all around us. Forty-nine of our 50 states now embrace state standards. All 49 will administer their own statewide standards-driven assessments by the spring of 2000. "The trend is to add more subjects and more grade levels to the tests, to test more often, and to attach higher stakes to the results" (Scherer, 1999, p. 5).

A standard is much more. It is a level to which to aspire.

When?

The struggle to develop a modern educational system that keeps pace with society's needs has been long and difficult. Standards-based reform has been at issue in some form for decades. It has consistently been a political football ever since America's educational system began to fall seriously behind the evolving needs of its population (and behind the quality of learning available to the citizens of other nations)—a fact which was raised so forcefully by the 1983 *A Nation at Risk*, the National Commission on Excellence in Education report. The issues surrounding the need for an implementation of standards are many and varied. Three of the major points of contention bear mentioning before we proceed to a chronology that puts the major events in historical perspective.

- **Standards—A Constitutional Issue.** Historically, the federal government has not sought to mandate or regulate the quality level of its citizens' education except for specific limited application issues involving equity, access to higher education, and research and statistics. In 1970, the founding fathers' deference to the states for educational matters was finally codified in public law. "No . . . department . . . of the United States (shall) exercise any direction, supervision, or control over the curriculum (or) administration . . . of any section educational institutions" (PL 103-33, General Education Provisions Act, section 432). Funding and control of educational issues has always rested with the states, who, until recently, have largely delegated that responsibility down to local governments.

- **Educational Requirements.** Only with the technological revolution in the latter half of this century has America's workplace needed more than basic rote learning in a limited number of core historical subject areas from its educational system.

- **"Old" versus "New" Standards.** Historically, the limited number of texts, simplified educational requirements for teachers, and low public knowledge expectations set by a largely agrarian and industrial society kept the notion of standards at a relatively-simple-to-achieve level. Today's educational requirements are driven by lightning-speed technological advances, a global market, and the consequent need for a widespread, highly trained, technology-based work force. Educational standards are highly complex and must be both content rich and capable of turning out a "product"—the educated student—with critical thinking and processing skills.

Educational standards are highly complex and must be both content rich and capable of turning out a "product"—the educated student—with critical thinking and processing skills.

Chronology: Origins of the Push for Educational Standards

Period	Dates	Comments
Era of Rudimentary Standards	1776–1950	–Localized economy and society largely agrarian (18th & 19th century) and industry (19th & early 20th century) –Few textbooks –Relatively low teacher training –Public education: simple, straightforward, usually rote learning centered, generally unsophisticated
Period of Technological Awakening	1950–1970	–Technology accelerating from World War II aftermath, and Cold War driven –General public education system remains largely stagnant –Heightened popularity of higher education –Introduction of widespread standardized testing
Public Education's Age of Awareness	1970–1990	
	1970	–General Education Provisions Act mandates federal government's continued exclusion from public education
	1975	–College board releases statistics documenting marked decline in student performance on SAT exams since 1963
	1975–1985	–Numerous local, state, and national level reports document widespread inadequacies in public education
	1983	–*A Nation at Risk* released by the National Commission on Excellence in Education at

		request of U.S. Secretary of Education, Terrell Bell
		• "The" headline report in both influence and media attention
		• Warned that U.S. educational foundations "are presently being eroded by a rising tide of mediocrity that threatens our future. . . ."
		• Recommendations:
		1. Higher standards (students and teachers)
		2. Establish a H.S. core curriculum
		3. Raise H.S. graduation standards
		4. Raise college entrance standards
		5. Lengthen school day and year
		6. Higher teacher salaries
	1983–1990	–Numerous early education reform attempts
		–Public attention and political consensus focusing on problems and alternative solutions
		–Numerous state-level initiatives focus on versions of content standards to establish what children are expected to learn/accomplish
Standards for the Millennium and the Age of Accountability	1990s	
	1989	–National Council of Teachers of Mathematics publishes national content standards for math
	1989–1990	–President Bush and the governors of all 50 states agree on a comprehensive plan to

	establish first ever national goals and voluntary standards, the *Goals 2000 Plan* (goals follow this section)
1991–1992	–U.S. Department of Education established grants to fund development of voluntary national standards in specific subject areas by national education groups and organizations
1994	–Goals 2000—Education American Act signed by President Clinton
	–Creates National Education Standards and Improvement Council (NESIC) to certify national standards being developed privately
	–Creates National Education Goals Panel (NEGP) to monitor standards development
	–Rejects concept of national assessment
1995	–American Federation of Teachers reports 49 of 50 states are pursuing standards-based reform
1996	–Second Education summit: President Clinton, 40 governors, 45 business and industry leaders

As of 1999, Goals 2000 and subsequent legislation has helped virtually all the states develop comprehensive content standards. Progress in establishing performance standards has been considerably less, with fewer than half the states completing development. Although now ten years old, the issue and process of developing standards as the definitive method of assessing (tracking) student achievement is still young. False starts and stumbles have occurred and can be expected because of the debate and politicizing of this issue by the democracy in which we live. Perhaps the Fordham Foundation (p. 1) expressed best our progress to date in its 1998 report on the state of state standards:

The "state of state standards" may be bleak, yet there is reason for hope. Fifteen years ago, when we declared A Nation at Risk, standards were non-existent and standards-based reform was a concept that few understood. Today, we have some solid standards and a widening consensus that standards-based reform is the kind of reform that U.S. education needs—and a necessary complement to reinventing public education. Yes, there's some blood on the floor. But there is progress, too. We might even be winning.

> Today, we have some solid standards and a widening consensus that standards-based reform is the kind of reform that U.S. education needs.

Goals 2000: National Education Goals

1. School Readiness. By the year 2000, all children in America will start school ready to learn.

2. School Completion. By the year 2000, the high school graduation rate will increase to at least 90 percent.

3. Student Achievement and Citizenship. By the year 2000, all students will leave grades 4, 8, and 12 having demonstrated competency over challenging subject matter including English, mathematics, science, foreign languages, civics and government, economics, arts, history, and geography; and every school in America will ensure that all students learn to use their minds well, so they may be prepared for responsible citizenship, further learning, and productive employment in our nation's modern economy.

4. Teacher Education and Professional Development. By the year 2000, the nation's teaching force will have access to programs for the continued improvement of their professional skills and the opportunity to acquire the knowledge and skills needed to instruct and prepare all American students for the next century.

5. Mathematics and Science. By the year 2000, United States undergraduates and graduate students, especially women and minorities, who complete degrees in mathematics, science, and engineering will increase significantly.

6. Adult Literacy and Lifelong Learning. By the year 2000, every adult American will be literate and will possess the knowledge and skills necessary to compete in a global economy and exercise the rights and responsibilities of citizenship.

7. Safe, Disciplined, and Alcohol- and Drug-Free Schools. By the year 2000, every school in the United States will be free of drugs, violence, and the unauthorized presence of firearms and alcohol and will offer a disciplined environment conducive to learning.

8. Parental Participation. By the year 2000, every school shall promote partnerships that will increase parental involvement and participation in promoting the social, emotional, and academic growth of children.

As adopted by Congress in March 1994, as part of the *Goals 2000: Educate America Act.*

Why?

As discussed in the introduction, standards of all sorts surround us in our daily lives. The purposes of standards range from protection to advancement. We speak of "meeting" standards, of achieving a level of proficiency sufficient to advance student knowledge. Standards have a positive connotation. They define achievement and raise expectations.

Part of defining achievement is the notion of direction. Standards provide a way for all stakeholders to see the destination and head that way. Most standards documents do not dictate how to arrive at the destination, so navigating from where we are to where we want to be is a matter of local preference. Even though we may choose different roads that have a variety of speed limits, curves, intersections, rest stops, and points of interest, we are all heading for the same destination.

In the world of education, standards represent desirable learning outcomes. They give us ways to measure success. Standards and standards-based assessment provide means for holding students, schools, districts, and states accountable for what occurs within our public schools.

Perhaps the most compelling answer to the "Why?" question is that standards provide high expectations for all students. In the absence of standards, educational opportunities are likely to be stratified according to where students live and what their backgrounds are. Because our society also tends to be stratified along racial and eco-

Standards provide a way for all stakeholders to see the destination and head that way.

nomic lines, many students are exposed to less-than-optimal educational opportunities (French, D. 1998).

Tucker and Codding (1998, p. 33) contend that " . . . the single most important obstacle to high student achievement in the United States is our low expectations for students—not just students who are poor and come from minority backgrounds but . . . most of our students." Setting the same high standards for all students helps ensure quality of opportunity. The standards provide for access to the same curriculum taught by qualified teachers. When schools are held accountable for the achievement of the same high standards, then all students will have the opportunity to take critical gatekeeping courses that prepare them for college and careers (Ravitch, 1995).

How?

As with any change, there are more questions than answers as we move into the era of content and performance standards. Chapters 2-8 will attempt to explore answers to some of the questions inherent in standards-based school reform. The following questions will be explored:

- How can we make standards part of our existing curriculum?
- How do we mesh what we know about learning with the requirements of standards?
- How can I enhance my instruction to best help my students master standards?
- How can we best prepare students for standard-based assessment?
- How can I organize my record keeping system to effectively keep track of student progress?
- How can districts and states help move students toward mastery of standards?
- How can the standards movement succeed?

How can standards be a part of existing curriculum?

Your state or district sends out heavy boxes to your school labeled "open immediately for distribution." It has happened before—new programs, new dictates, more work. But this time it is different. The standards documents in the boxes represent a fundamental change in how we approach education. This movement will not fade (Willis, 1997). State standards must be taken seriously, but they need not be viewed as completely disruptive in terms of what we teach and expect children to learn in our classrooms.

Figuring out the changes that need to occur in terms of curriculum will hopefully be a group project, by team or by grade level. In the absence of a support group, individual teachers may find themselves struggling through the process. Here are some suggestions and comments that may make the process easier.

The standards documents in the boxes represent a fundamental change in how we approach education.

11

1. A comparison of state standards and existing curriculum must be done. Often districts will take care of this step through central office staff or committees of teachers. If not, considerable time will be needed for this first and crucial step. Here's how you might go about it.

   • Obtain local curriculum documents for each subject/grade.

   • No matter how long you have taught the prescribed curriculum, take another look—an objective overview. Look at the curriculum in a holistic way, and then look at details.

   • Read through the entire grade/subject level with which you will work, plus the grade level before and the one after. For instance, if you teach fifth grade, read the entire language arts curriculum for fourth, fifth, and sixth grades. It is important to follow a standard from where your students have been to where they are going.

   • Now compare. It is generally easier to view a strand from the standards and find levels of alignment in the curriculum unless you teach basically from one text or resource. Most teachers pull materials from a variety of sources, and the standards help bring organization and structure.

   • Most teachers find the curricular content of their state standards a good match for their regular curriculum. If this is the case, the major concern may be the format in which the content is presented.

   • If the state standards go into greater depth than your curriculum in a content area, it will be necessary to expand your curriculum in the particular area to match the state standards. This is critical information to know.

   • If your curriculum, on the other hand, is broader or conveys a topic in more depth, then decisions need to be made about priorities. Do you keep something in your curriculum that is not a part of mandated state standards? In this day of high stakes accountability, do you want to spend time on a topic that will not be assessed by your state? The topic may be assessed on a national norm-referenced test, however. Your district may make the decision for you. If not, weigh priorities and time demands.

Once you have achieved alignment, relative weightings need to be determined. For instance, if you teach seventh grade geography and have traditionally spent one-fourth of the school year on the geography of Europe, but your state standards, while certainly including Europe, only indicate about one-tenth of the standards will specifically deal with European geography, then changes need to be made—changes in emphasis, not the wholesale removal of entire units. We all also have "pet content" that we enjoy. There are books and materials we are comfortable with and like to use in our classrooms. As long as there is reasonable alignment between the topics/content we teach and the standards, we are fine. But remember that adjustments never have to be black and white. Keep portions of your "pet content"!

2. Some standards are written in vague, global teams. We need to keep in mind that standards are *ends*. How we get to those ends are our means. Chances are that the standards will organize our content. They will provide the Roman numerals and capital letters of our content outline. The details of how we get from one major point to the next is up to us. Established content lessons and units may easily serve as conduit.

3. Teachers usually have the freedom to sequence topics and content as they please. Standards rarely dictate the order in which topics are taught. Certainly within topics, order of detailed coverage is not mandated. So we have topics and levels of specificity, but generally the time line will be up to us. Rather than feeling "put upon" by sequencing demands, teachers can experience the freedom, as they have traditionally, to make decisions about when, and usually how, curriculum takes shape in their classrooms.

4. Some districts will choose to make the actual standards their curriculum. This can either satisfy the whole alignment issue, or cause teachers to revamp and replan. Of course, it is not reasonable to ask teachers to completely change what they do in the classroom. Be assured that no state has adopted standards that would require drastic measures in terms of either content inclusion or revision.

Some districts will choose to make the actual standards their curriculum.

We have often heard that *how* we teach is as important as *what* we teach. When it comes to fulfilling the mandate of state standards, what we are to teach and what students are expected to learn are defined for us. So the "what" is set, while the "how" is left to us to determine according to student learning styles and needs. In the early stages of standards implementation, we need a curriculum that aligns with and embraces standards. In the absence of some of the standards in our regular curriculum, those standards may be rewritten to reflect even more strongly the knowledge and skills that are found in our state standards.

How do learning theories mesh with standards?

Standards-based instruction needs to take advantage of what is known about how the brain works.

One of the hottest fields in educational research deals with how the brain works. What motivates, captivates, and endures in the brain determines to large extent what and how we learn. There are characteristics of how the brain processes and assimilates knowledge that we may have activated intuitively in the past, but now there are researchers who have made it their life's work to understand these characteristics. Some of the needs of the learners are predetermined by the very nature of the brain (Gunter, Estes & Schwab, 1999). Standards-based instruction needs to take advantage of what is known about how the brain works. Caine and Caine describe 12 principles of brain-based learning. They have major implications for what teachers do in classrooms. The italicized words are Caine and Caine's principles. The comments are this author's.

Caine and Caine 12 Principles

1. *The brain is a parallel processor.* Teaching content and skill in isolation fights this principle. The brain can do more than one thing at once! We certainly know this is true of teachers. We should remember that our students' brains work the same way. Parallel processing capabilities allow students to learn from what they see, hear, and do—all at the same time. This has

14

implications for interdisciplinary instruction since the brain can also employ multiple sensors. Students working in a group to construct a medieval castle can absorb medieval music and glance up at medieval art displayed around the room all at once. This principle tells us that educational posters on the wall are a good idea for learning, not just attractive decorations.

2. *Learning engages the entire physiology.* The natural energy of children can work for us as teachers rather than at odds with what we are trying to accomplish in the classroom. Learning is a function of the brain and takes place at every level, consciously or subconsciously.

3. *The search for meaning is innate.* Students want to learn. In fact, they cannot stop themselves. They are constantly looking for meaning. What wonderful potential! Students are not empty vessels, but rather are people with prior knowledge, and they want more! As teachers, we must shape their world to allow for the natural bent toward learning so they will have meaningful directions and connections.

> **Students want to learn. In fact, they cannot stop themselves.**

4. *The search for meaning occurs through patterning.* Finding patterns requires making connections among old and new knowledge and skills. On a smaller scale, patterning involves finding the missing numbers in a sequence, identifying patterns in behavior among elected officials, discovering patterns that occur in nature, creating patterns in writing genres, etc. Generally children are good at this skill, but most will recognize and create patterns at a more rapid pace if they are encouraged to do so, are shown examples, and are fortunate to have a teacher who models the search for patterns.

5. *Emotions are crucial to learning the skill of patterning.* If meaning comes through patterning, and patterning comes more easily when emotions are positive towards the activity, then teachers need to spend time on the affective component of the teacher/student, student/knowledge, and student/skills relationships. Emotions matter! To make the most of a student's natural desire to learn, and to learn through patterning, the student's motivation and desire make a difference.

6. *The brain simultaneously processes parts and wholes.* Students are able to see the big picture and the individual parts at the same time. There is no need to segregate the two. Using the inductive processes involved in inquiry learning remains an excellent way to facilitate discovery. Long ago, teachers observed that while all the specifics of a topic are

being discovered, the overriding generalizations that students need to grasp is being assimilated at the same time.

7. *Learning involves both focused attention and peripheral perception.* As with principle #1, this principle speaks volumes concerning what we do with all of those "atmospheric" components. Some educators believe that everything that happens at school comprises the curriculum. This principle supports this belief and encourage teachers to pay close attention to all aspects of their school, and particularly their classrooms.

8. *Learning always involves conscious and unconscious processes.* Sometimes the unconscious part of learning cannot be hurried. The conscious aspect of the brain may hear presentations, see presentations, be involved in group work, and appear to have all the elements in place for learning. But if learning does not occur even with these elements in place, this principle tells us that there may be unconscious elements at work. Time for reflection may be needed, or time needs to be allowed simply for a concept to "sink in."

9. *We have at least two different types of memory: a spatial memory system and a set of systems for rote learning.* Spatial memory requires very little, if any, rehearsal. What is in spatial memory is truly "owned." It takes no effort to recall what is in spatial memory. It is a natural fit in circumstances where it is needed. Rote learning is learning that takes place on purpose. It requires effort and rehearsal. We assume certain levels of spatial memory exist for our students and on that, at least partially, we expect to build rote learning.

10. *We understand and remember best when facts and skills are embedded in natural, spatial memory.* To have something embedded in spatial memory usually implies that there was prior knowledge or connections already in place. Spatial memory is three dimensional and what it contains closely aligns with the functioning of everyday life.

11. *Learning is enhanced by challenge and inhibited by threat.* All learning in the classroom should be reviewed in terms of opportunity with an element of challenge. If school and learning and exploration are perceived in a positive way, then learning is enhanced. If, on the other hand, content and skills are presented as a "do or die" kind of threat, this principle tells us that the brain will resist. If our definition for learning is a narrow one, threats may work. If our definition of learning involves embracing knowledge and skills, then being challenged, and therefore learning, will lead us to "own" rather than "borrow" knowledge and skills.

Some educators believe that everything that happens at school comprises the curriculum.

---

12. *Each brain is unique.* It is not the purpose or intent of standards documents to dictate pedagogy. Standards, as outcomes, tell us where we are going and what our goals are. The instructional strategies are up to us. Teachers are not restricted in teaching styles, just as students are not limited in learning styles. The fact that every brain is unique presents a challenge for teachers. In conjunction with principle #11, the teacher's own learning of his or her art/science of instruction is enhanced by the challenge of remembering that each student has a unique brain.

Tucker and Codding (1998) present five basic principles of learning. Each one applies directly to classroom instruction. They should guide all that we do and have particular relevance given the structure of content and skills presented in state standards. We have our goals. Understanding more about how learning takes place and is enhanced will help us reach this goal.

Principles of Learning (Tucker & Codding, pp. 76–80)

1. *Student effort is a more important determinant of achievement than natural ability.* The American idea that the most important factor in explaining educational achievement is inherited ability is simply wrong. Most students can achieve at what most of us would regard as very high levels if they work hard enough at it.

2. *Getting all students to achieve at high levels depends on clear expectations that are the same for all students.*

3. *All students need a thinking curriculum—one that provides a deep understanding of the subject and the ability to apply that understanding to the complex, real-world problems that the student will face as an adult.*

4. *Students of all ages learn best in two types of circumstances: when they are seeking and using knowledge and skills to address problems that challenge and engage them, and when they are teaching others.* We learn well when we are hanging the new knowledge on something we already know, when we see the connections to things we know and care about, when we can use the new knowledge to do something that we need or want to do.

5. *People learn well when working beside an expert who models skilled practice and encourages and guides learners as they create products or performances for audiences whose reactions really matter.*

> **Standards, as outcomes, tell us where we are going and what our goals are.**

17

How can instruction be enhanced to help students master standards?

Standards-based
instruction can be
many things to many
students, depending
upon their grade and
ability levels.

All the curriculum alignment in the world will not affect student learning without conscious and purposeful consideration of instructional practices. While traditional methods of lecture, question/answer, group work, etc., are all appropriate, there are ways to "tweak" our instruction to enhance its effectiveness. Understanding the purposes of standards and the potential impact of making the students fully aware of what standards are and how they shape learning will cause us to rethink instructional strategies. Standards-based instruction can be many things to many students, depending upon their grade and ability levels.

1. As teachers, we must understand our state standards fully. They are written in language familiar to us. The bits of jargon and the subject-specific references are second nature. The words conjure up examples and connections because we see the big picture and have worked with curriculum rhetoric since our pre-service training. Just because we teach first grade and the neighbor down the street teaches junior high language arts, we do not understand the jargon in different ways. The applications are certainly different, but a high school student could read a set of standards and grasp a good portion of it. They may need little or no interpretation to understand what expectations are implied. An elementary school student, however, will most likely need an explanation in more concrete language, accompanied by relevant examples, to know what is expected. Middle school students tend to be all over the board when it comes to the ability to grasp both literal and abstract concepts.

Standards are written for teachers in language teachers understand. *It is our responsibility to translate and interpret standards into appropriate "student language."* That language will vary according to grade level/ability level. We know our students and are in the best position to provide the appropriate explanations. Remember that most students will not understand or embrace phrases like "to demonstrate proficiency in interpreting a passage!"

2. As made clear in the previous chapter about the principles of learning, students benefit greatly from exposure to concepts and skills. Just as we would post math formulas, word walls, steps of the scientific method, etc., *posters and reminders concerning standards are very appropriate.* Students need an awareness of our expectations in order to achieve them. Visual reminders of the standards can be approached in the same manner as classroom objectives many teachers write on the chalkboard under the day's date.

3. To make standards an accepted part of education—things like cooperative learning, vocabulary lists, quizzes, etc.—they must become part of our common language. It is true that children will develop habits, with or without teachers. Left to their own devices, student habits may form that are less than desirable. The wise teacher understands this and wants a hand in the development of school-related habits to make the routines of the day run smoothly. That same teacher will help students make standards a "habit" in that they become part of the habitual common language of the classroom. Knowing that a standard is attached to a lesson (or even several standards) should become as expected as the routine of where to write one's name and date on an assignment. *Talk to students about standards.* Weave them into classroom conversations.

4. Along with visual and auditory reference and reminders of standards in and around the classroom, take this principle an important step further. Include standards in everything you ask students to learn. Make this just as natural as writing or saying, "This assignment is due Tuesday." *On every worksheet, set of questions, math drill, cooperative group task—whatever the assignment—write a relevant standard.* While this may seem awkward and even contrived, it makes the point that there are reasons for what we do, and those reasons build on one another as learning takes its course. The pleasant, and perhaps unexpected, teacher treat is that students will not only come to expect a standard to be assigned to what they do, they will actually become quite

It is our responsibility to translate and interpret standards into appropriate "student language."

good at determining target standards themselves! Just imagine what it would be like to teach sixth grade science and have the students know and be able to verbalize the standards they mastered as fifth graders and be able to tell you the next logical progression the skill or content might take in your sixth grade classroom. Can you imagine the implications of students knowing where they have been in a particular standard strand and either know or be able to logically anticipate the next layer of learning! We surely would have learners actively involved in their own learning.

5. We now have standards that are interpreted appropriately for students, as well as visual and auditory reminders that are embedded in our routines and more reminders included in all we present and ask students to discover and learn. But what does it mean to master a standard? What does student work that shows mastery look like? How will students know when they have "made it," when they have accomplished what we want them to? Not showing samples of standards that are met is tantamount to asking students to shoot a basket on a basketball court when the hoop is on the other side of a wall. It is difficult to aim without a target in sight! The old adage "A picture is worth a thousand words" rings true when it comes to standards-based instructions. We can describe mastery work, we can give directions, students can practice according to our descriptions and directions, but nothing illustrates a target quite like a sample of what mastery look like. These samples are often referred to as exemplars. According to Harris and Carr (1996, pp. 40–41), exemplars serve three major functions:

   1. Exemplars of student work help to ensure fair and consistent feedback to students by providing a stable reference point across students and over time. The practice of referring to these papers when scoring or grading student work helps to ensure consistency in scoring (psychometricians refer to this as reliability).

   2. Exemplars give students a clear view of the target. If you share performance, descriptive, and related exemplars of student work with students in advance, students can—and do—begin to evaluate their own work in relation to the standards.

   3. Exemplars are useful in communicating with parents. Performance descriptions alone are seldom detailed enough to allow parents to visualize the desired result. Examples of student work define acceptable and unacceptable levels of performance in a concrete and meaningful way for parents and others who are concerned about student progress.

What does student work that shows mastery look like?

20

In language arts, asking students to write a colorful description of an event and explaining that we want them to use interesting words may illicit something beyond "the sky was dark and scary," but possibly not. If we want colorful, robust language, we need to model what we mean. To do this we would give directions and then provide an example such as "The black sky enveloped him with debilitating fear." Discuss why this sentence is more colorful and interesting than the first. Now the students are ready to try it themselves. With this kind of lesson, peer opinions of the relative colorfulness of each sentence drive home the concept of color in language. Have students make suggestions, write, and then rewrite.

Standards-based instruction in math can be approached similarly. Problem solving involves both concept knowledge and computation skills. Until recently, teachers asked students to simply come up with a correct answer. Thanks in part to the National Council of Teachers of Mathematics, most states, and therefore teachers in those states, realize the rich possibilities of conceptual learning that exist within each problem-solving scenario. Teachers understand the value of students showing process and then writing a narrative to explain the thinking that leads to the process and the product. Peer conversation about process can also facilitate learning. A student-written explanation should be understandable to another student. Encourage students to talk to one another about how they think about a problem solving scenario. Then allow time for students to rethink and redo their process and explanation.

Teachers understand the value of students showing process and then writing a narrative to explain the thinking that leads to the process and the product.

These principles apply to all subjects. Here is a recap of the preceding two paragraphs.

Teachers should do the following:

- give descriptions of mastery and directions for assignment
- show what mastery looks like
- allow time for students to work
- support peer conversations
- give time for rewriting and reworking

Another effective way to let students know what mastery looks like involves rubrics. A rubric is a scoring guide that indicates the criteria for evaluating student work. Rubrics give descriptions for levels of proficiency, accuracy, and quality that allow students to know if their work shows no evidence of mastery, meets the standards of mastery, or exceeds the standard.

The efficacy of using a thematic approach to curriculum and instruction—to teaching and learning—is not news to teachers. Both Tucker and Codding's Principles of Learning and Caine and Caine's Principles of Brain-Based Learning confirm that making connections of prior knowledge and new knowledge, as well as new concepts connecting to other new concepts, promotes learning. It is likely that every teacher reading this book has developed and/or implemented some form of interdisciplinary instruction. Even before we had the educational jargon to go with the concept, we intuitively knew to promote connections.

Now we need to make sure the standards we are given for our students make their way into interdisciplinary units that we already regularly use or into units that we have yet to develop. As we examine this area of the teaching/learning cycle we will once again realize that most of what is in the standards documents is not new, perhaps just better articulated and organized.

A distinction has been made in the literature between an activity-based unit and a standards-based unit. Take a long look at the following chart.

Comparing Activity-Based and Standards-Based Units of Study

Activity-Based Units	Standards-Based Units
Activities are the means and the ends.	Activities are the means and standards are the ends.
Activities are selected based on relationship to topic or essential questions and fit with other unit activities.	Activities are selected based on their usefulness in helping students learn and demonstrate attainment of knowledge and skill in identified standards.
Assessment is based on expectations for particular products or performances (e.g., graph is properly labeled).	Assessment is based on criteria that is directly related to standards (e.g., knowledge of necessary content and concepts, or the ability to comprehend or to use specific steps in a problem-solving process).
Communication with students, parents, and other teachers about student's progress tends to be about activities and expectations.	Communication with students, parents, and other teachers about student progress is based on standards.

Reading the elements on the chart from Harris and Carr (1996, p. 15) may evoke comments such as "Yes, I see myself and my units as a little of both." Please don't feel offended if you see more of yourself on the left. Try it this way—instead of the word "standards" on the right, read in the words "knowledge and skills of the curriculum." Feel better?

Aligning what we do in our classrooms with standards-based education does not mean throwing out what works. It requires, rather, perhaps a new way of thinking about what we do. We have very distinct outcomes—namely the standards. We can take a unit of study and attach standards to it. If there are activities or assignments to which we cannot find a standard, it may be time to rethink the "why" of what we have previously done. The standards are our priorities. We should act accordingly, revising an existing unit involves specific questions. We again turn to Harris and Carr (1996).

Aligning what we do in our classrooms with standards-based education does not mean throwing out what works.

- What standards does the unit address?
- What activities should be added to ensure students' success in attaining standards?
- Which activities are not central to attaining the standards? Should those activities be dropped?
- Do the identified standards address impact, process, content, rule, or form, or do additional standards need to be added to achieve balance and focus the unit?
- If standards are added, do you need to add more activities to support students in attaining these standards?
- Considering the unit as a whole, are the activities doable, or should some be changed or omitted?

Writing an interdisciplinary unit of study involves some straightforward steps, none of which should be bypassed. As you read through these steps, recall the components of a standards-based unit as stated on the chart. The standards should infuse each step as we consider themes, activities, guiding questions, generalizations, assessment, products, performances, and all forms of communication.

Creating an interdisciplinary unit:

1. **Choose a theme.** This theme may be based on content (i.e., an event, object, or other tangible phenomenon). The theme may also be based on a concept—a broader, more abstract approach that allows for connections under a larger umbrella of though. It is important that the theme be generative, that it leads to questions and exploration. Examples of concepts as

themes include celebrating differences, cause and effect, civil disobedience, and change.

Themes may come from a variety of sources. They may come directly from a standard or a combination of standards. They may be topical. For instance, the sixth grade curriculum in social studies may be ancient civilizations. A theme may be "rivers," with a focus on the Nile and the Ganges and how civilizations used these rivers. Taking the theme to a conceptual level may mean changing the theme from "rivers" to "navigations." The rivers themselves are still important, but the unit takes on a broader perspective to include man's ingenuity to find his way on water, on land, and even philosophically. Either approach, content or concept, can be developed in rich ways to be both inclusive of standards and fascinating to students and teachers.

... good questions should guide instruction.

2. **Decide on generalizations.** Out of every unit of study there are indisputable (or practically indisputable!) generalizations that can be made. These are the absolutes we want students to know and be able to verbalize and defend. For instance, a unit on celebrating differences may include generalizations such as the following:

• Differences exist among people. This generalization can be supported through scientific inquiry, examples from history, statistics on an almost endless number of dimensions, etc.

• People are often judgmental about differences. Again we can turn to statistics concerning any number of prejudices. We can read about having judgmental attitudes in all forms of literature. We can find historical evidence in every generation.

Whatever generalizations we decide on as teachers, we need to be ready to add more as our students grapple with issues.

3. **Develop guiding questions.** Whether you call it inquiry learning or constructivist theory or the Socratic method, good questions should guide instruction. A unit of study should be framed by explorations. Teachers should not fall victim to the "ask a question, no one answers in five seconds, give the answer" syndrome. Remember Tucker and Codding's Principle of Learning #4 (p. 78) that says, "Students of all ages learn best . . . when they are seeking and using knowledge and skills to address problems that challenge and engage them." That is the point of well thought out questions.

4. **Web the theme.** An interdisciplinary team of teachers has the potential to make a unit of study one big bundle of connections. Everyone involved should brainstorm and contribute and enrich a theme. If an interdisciplinary team is not a part of our organized structure, grade-level groups of teachers can get

together. If you are, or feel, isolated and teach all or almost all of the subjects to your group of students, invite creative folks to join you in the "thinking stages" of unit development. The planning wheel from Teaching at the Middle Level (129) is an excellent guide.

Curricular Connections Planning Wheel

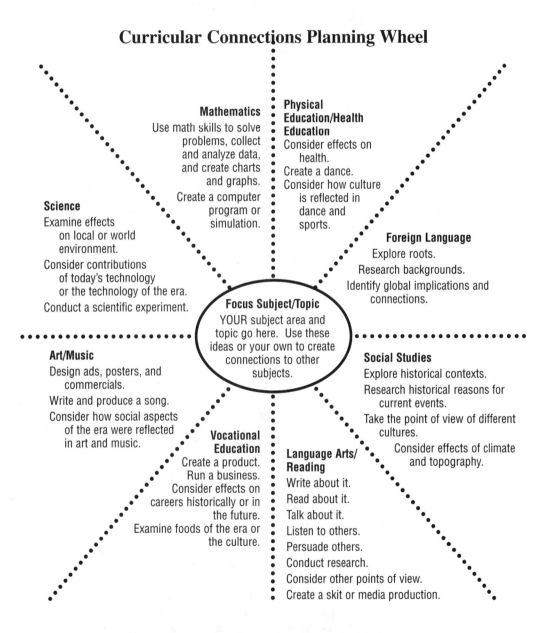

Mathematics
Use math skills to solve problems, collect and analyze data, and create charts and graphs.
Create a computer program or simulation.

Physical Education/Health Education
Consider effects on health.
Create a dance.
Consider how culture is reflected in dance and sports.

Science
Examine effects on local or world environment.
Consider contributions of today's technology or the technology of the era.
Conduct a scientific experiment.

Foreign Language
Explore roots.
Research backgrounds.
Identify global implications and connections.

Focus Subject/Topic
YOUR subject area and topic go here. Use these ideas or your own to create connections to other subjects.

Art/Music
Design ads, posters, and commercials.
Write and produce a song.
Consider how social aspects of the era were reflected in art and music.

Social Studies
Explore historical contexts.
Research historical reasons for current events.
Take the point of view of different cultures.
Consider effects of climate and topography.

Vocational Education
Create a product.
Run a business.
Consider effects on careers historically or in the future.
Examine foods of the era or the culture.

Language Arts/Reading
Write about it.
Read about it.
Talk about it.
Listen to others.
Persuade others.
Conduct research.
Consider other points of view.
Create a skit or media production.

Developed by Joan M. Palmer, Howard County Public School System, Maryland.

5. **Plan large-group and schedule-changing events (activities).** This is common sense. Anything that takes us outside the classroom or requires rearranging of schedules needs to be done well in advance for reasons of courtesy to others affected such as transportation needs, cafeteria staff and the grounds crew.

6. **Plan beginning and culminating activities.** These make or break a unit. Getting the attention of students, creating interest, awakening curiosity—without this component, a unit will "die on the vine," and be nothing more than a perfunctory exercise. Celebrating what has been learned and accomplished in a "big splash" culminating event focuses why the unit was developed. Make a detailed list of all the standards encompassed in the unit along with evidence of student mastery. Proudly display the list. Communicate it to parents and educators alike. This is the payoff! Invite participation in the culminating event where students display products and give performances to show what they know and can do. Parents, community members, building administrators, other teachers, and other students—let them all know what you and your students have been up to!

7. **Detail daily plans in all areas.** There is a variety of ways of doing this. Teaches write plans, share them, look for gaps and overlaps, modify, make decisions about team teaching, suggest how standards may be better incorporated, etc. If you have a self-contained elementary classroom, many of these steps may be accomplished as solo endeavors.

8. **Plan and combine assessments to reflect standards in a variety of formats.** A major test at the end of a unit will not measure the learning that has taken place. Assessments built into activities utilizing observation, product scoring rubrics, checklists for steps in ongoing projects, intermittent content quizzes, etc., measure progress and provide opportunities for frequent feedback to students. Remember to frame assessments in terms of standards in ways that give students clear objectives.

9. **Enjoy the unit!** Be both a daily participant with your students as you take pleasure in all the phases and also be an "out of body" participant in that you mentally step away to see the big picture of how the unit is contributing to the learning of your students.

10. **Reflect, document, and evaluate the unit.** Keep a detailed journal of everything involved in the unit. List resources (books, magazines, community members, organizations, Web sites, etc.). Be critical of each phase, activity, and assessment. Indicate what worked and what did not. Label everything with the standards that are addressed, and be sure to do it across disciplines. Ask everyone touched by the unit to evaluate it in

some fashion. This can be accomplished with formal surveys, conversations, or general questions posed in writing or verbally. Folks to include are other teachers, the principal, guest speakers, parents, people involved in field trips, and, of course, the students themselves.

Teacher Created Materials offers a wealth of information to help in the planning and implementation of interdisciplinary units from general guidelines for the process to ready-made units and activities to software that utilizes existing technology.

Here are some suggestions:

- Professional's Guide—Integrated Thematic Units
- Thematic Units Using Technology (complete, in-depth units with technology skills and a huge supply of appendices)
- Thematic Units for early childhood, primary, intermediate, and middle grades, based on science, social studies, and literature themes
- books on using newspapers, the Internet, holidays, major events, multiple intelligences, etc.
- *Standards: Meeting Them in the Classroom.* These are a MUST! A series of three books (one for primary, intermediate, and challenging levels); each is full of ideas for addressing standards in the classroom.

How can students prepare for standards-based assessment?

For years, our students have taken standardized tests, mostly norm-referenced tests purchased from national publishers. Students are used to the routine and accustomed to the format, which is typically multiple choice. Now here come standards. And where there are state standards, there will surely be specialized assessments to match the standards. The alignment between standards and assessment is the ideal that not all states have achieved. Schmoker and Marzano (1999) reviewed state standards documents and believe that many of them will never be thoroughly assessed. There is simply too much in the documents to test. What a state chooses to include on their assessment reflects priorities of standards. By the third or fourth year, teachers and students can become comfortable with these priorities. If it is the first year for state standards-based assessment, then what the assessment reflects is more than likely anyone's guess!

Standards call for new forms of assessment. Student performance requires more authentic forms that go beyond multiple choice and short answer formats.

Most states provide, or are in the process of developing, sample test items that are available to classroom teachers. Take advantage of them! If there are five sample items developed for third grade math, they can serve as patterns for teachers to use to write parallel items. Even if curricular content has not changed significantly due to standards, it is likely that the format of some of the items will be different from traditional tests. This format/expectation change is important. For instance, math items that traditionally asked for a single answer may now ask for the answer *plus* a narrative explanation. Or items may be multi-layered. Our students may not be accustomed to these differences. Writing parallel items will help familiarize them with the new expectations. Many states have written rubrics for math items. This is a very recent innovation. What follows is the math rubric used in Pennsylvania. In general, the Pennsylvania standards and assessments are thoroughly developed.

Mathematics—General Rubric

5: Advanced Understanding, Excellent

- A category "5" response represents correct procedures, correct calculations and a written explanation which fully supports all the work shown.

  Excellence is shown through exemplary work and explanation which make it clear that the student fully understands the concepts involved in the solution process. For certain tasks, the student may demonstrate advanced understanding through providing an alternate solution or more than one correct answer.

4: Satisfactory Understanding

- A category "4" response represents a correct answer with correct procedures, correct calculations, and a written explanation which supports the works shown and demonstrates a satisfactory level of understanding.

3: Almost Satisfactory Understanding

- A category "3" response is:
  1. The correct answer, with incomplete calculations, procedures or explanation; OR
  2. The correct answer, with correct and complete calculations, procedures or explanation, but with incorrect labeling: OR
  3. The incorrect (mechanics) procedure along with correct explanation, but made one calculation or copying error which was through the correct solution procedure, thereby resulting in an incorrect answer.

2: Partial Understanding

- A category "2" response is:
  1. An incorrect answer which contains the necessary information (data, numbers, procedures, etc.) for solving the task without including irrelevant information in the solution process. Either the student did not proceed far enough or proceeded incorrectly.

     A procedure error is evident in the category to cause the incorrect answer, NOT a calculation error.
  2. An incorrect answer but has correct procedures and has made two calculation or copying errors.

1: Minimal Understanding

- A category "1" response is:

    1. A correct answer, but with calculations, procedures or explanations that are either not legible or not understandable or missing or the procedure is incorrect.

    2. No answer or an incorrect one, but the student has provided some of the information critical to the solution.

0: Incorrect Response

- A category "0" response is an incorrect answer in which the student attempts the task incorrectly or gives an incorrect or incomplete answer with an incorrect explanation or no explanation of the procedure of logic used in the solution.

- Blank responses and Off-Task responses are scored as "Incorrect Responses."

- Questions marks and "I don't know" are scored as "Incorrect Responses." The student has read or seen the task and responded to it.

B: Blank Response (No Response)

- A category "B" response is a blank page, where a student did not attempt the task and there is no indication that the student read the task. The answer sheet is a blank or an erased blank page.

- An erased page is no indication that the student has read the task or attempted it. The erased writing may not have related at all to the task.

OT: Off-Task Response, Irrelevant Response

- A category "OT" response is an off-task response, irrelevant response or a drawing, etc., that does not address anything within or about the task. Such a resonse gives no evidence that the student has even read the task.

From *The Mathematics Assessment Handbook*, PDE, Harrisburg, PA, 1998.

Now here is a sample practice item provided by Pennsylvania. The problem is followed by a solution and then a specific rubric. Notice the detail required for full credit.

Grade 8 Sample Task with Scoring Rubric

In a city, there are 50,000 cable TV subscribers. Recently, six hundred of them were randomly surveyed to determine their program preference. The results were as follows: 126 preferred comedy, 225 preferred sports, 193 preferred movies, and 56 named "other" as their #1 TV preference. Using the results of this survey, approximately how many of the total cable TV subscribers would be expected to identify sports as their program preference?

You must show each step of your math work and write an explanation describing the steps you followed to arrive at your answer and why you chose each step, even if you did mental math or used a calculator.

Problem Solution:

This problem can be solved in a variety of ways:

- Find the ratio of the viewers who prefer sports to the total surveyed group, then apply that ratio to the total population of 50,000 to find a figure of 18,750.

- Solve by using a proportional equation and arrive at 18,750 (preferably).

- Solve using percents (37.5% of 50,000 = 18,750) or proportions where the answers will vary according to rounding procedure used. (83.333 X 225 = 18,749.925 OR 83.3 X 225 = 18,742.5 OR 83 X 335 = 18,675) OR (rounding to 18,749.925 to 18,750 etc) OR (rounding to 19,000 or 20,000). A student may even answer "3 out of 8 subscribers."

5: Advanced Understanding

- A category "5" response represents a *correct answer with correct procedures, correct calculations, and a written explanation that supports the work shown* and the mathematical concepts used in the solution, thereby demonstrating an advanced level of understanding.

  1. This category shows an understanding beyond what is acceptable for a "Satisfactory Understanding" and the student clearly demonstrates advanced understanding of the work shown.

2. The main emphasis (beyond the correct answer and work shown) is the explanation of how and why the procedure was done. The written explanation must indicate to the scorer a firm understanding of the procedures used and not just written explanation of the first steps. (e.g., First add, then divide, then . . .) of the procedures used.

4: Satisfactory Understanding

- *Correct answer* of approximately 18,750 viewers prefer sports. Correct calculation, procedures, and written explanation shown.

3: Almost Satisfactory

- *Correct answer* with incomplete calculations, procedures, or written explanations shown.
- *Incorrect answer* with the correct procedures or explanation shown.

2: Partial Understanding

- *Incorrect answer* with the correct procedure or explanation with two calculations or copying errors.
- *Incorrect answer* but contains necessary information showing a correct ratio, proportion, or division for solving the problem with no calculation or copying error and either does not proceed any further or proceeds incorrectly.

1: Minimal Understanding

- *Correct answer*, but with calculations, procedures, or explanations that are either not legible, or not understandable, or missing or incorrect.
- *Incorrect or no answer* with correct procedures or explanations with 3 calculations or copying errors.
- *Incorrect or no answer* and has information such as a *correct* ratio, proportion, division with an appropriate procedure for solving the problem, and has a calculation or copying error.
- *Incorrect answer* but contains necessary information showing a *correct* ratio, proportion, or division for solving the problem with a calculation or copying error and either does not proceed any further or proceeds incorrectly.

0: Incorrect Response

- Incorrect response or incomplete response with incorrect or no explanation of the procedure or logic used in the solution.

From *The Mathematics Assessment Handbook*, PDE, Harrisburg, PA, 1998

Even if much of a standards-based assessment utilizes multiple choice items, there will likely be a writing assessment that will be scored using a rubric. Again, we turn to Pennsylvania for a sample rubric covering five characteristics of effective writing: focus, content, organization, style, and conventions. The Pennsylvania Holistic Scoring Guide has two components, the six-point scoring rubric and the five characteristics of effective writing: focus, content, organization, style, and conventions. The following is the six- point scoring rubric.

6	5	4	3	2	1
sharp, distinct focus	clear focus	adequate focus	vague focus	confused focus	absence of focus
substantial, specific, and/or illustrative content; sophisticated ideas that are particularly well developed	specific and illustrative content	sufficient content, appropriate organization	content limited to a listing, repetition, or mere sequence of ideas	superficial content	absence of relevant content
obviously controlled and/or subtle organization	logical and appropriate organization	some precision and variety is sentence structure and word choice	inconsistent organization	confused organization	absence of organization
writer's voice apparent in tone, sentence structure, and word choice	precision and variety in sentence structure and word choice	mechanical and usage errors not severe enough to interfere significantly with the writer's purpose	limited sentence variety and word choice	lack of sentence and word choice variety	no apparent control over sentence structure and word choice
few mechanical and usage errors	some mechanical and usage errors		repeated weaknesses in mechanics and usage	mechanical and usage errors that seriously interfere with the writer's purpose	mechanical and usage errors so severe that writer's ideas are difficult, if not impossible, to understand

Non-Scorable (NS)

– is illegible; i.e. includes so many undecipherable words that no sense can be made of the response

– is incoherent; i.e., words are legible but syntax is so garbled that response makes no sense

– is a blank paper

Off-Prompt (OF)

– is readable but did not respond to prompt.

In our classrooms, we can choose the types of assessment we use. To increase student flexibility, a wide variety is best. Harris and Carr (1996) caution against using a single source of evidence to judge attainment of a standard. They contend that multiple sources are needed to document the attainment of any one standard. They suggest that students build a portfolio of sources of evidence across time. Traditional assessment (involving multiple choice, true/false, matching, short answer, and essay) still has a role in our planned assessment. There are content areas and time constraints that dictate the use of traditional assessment tools. This is another case of not abandoning what we know is effective, but rather tempering the familiar with what we find to be equally, if not more, effective in terms of measuring what students know and can do. Projects, portfolios, performances—all requiring subjective scoring—tend to reflect the knowledge and skills emphasized by national organization standards and, subsequently, state standards. Subjective scoring involves two factors that make it more difficult: the need for a consistent quality criteria, and time.

Students need to see what acceptable levels of performance look like. Examples should be used to define acceptable and unacceptable student work. These examples are important for teachers and parents as they make judgments concerning what, if any, assistance is needed. Rubrics provide a consistent way to look at exemplars and student work to make judgments concerning quality. Comments such as "good," "nice work," "try it again," etc., are not sufficient to guide students toward standards mastery. Rubrics and exemplars provide both the language and the logic to apply these scoring tools to address student strengths and weaknesses. The time necessary to apply these scoring tools is undeniably greater than with most traditional assessments. Teacher time is already at a premium. Here is where a supportive administrative structure needs to spring into action. Creative scheduling that allows for greater planning time during the school day helps immensely. If teachers are expected to whole-heartedly embrace the kinds of assessment discussed here, the time must be found to allow them to do so.

"Standards-based assessment can be a powerful tool for you and your students." Harris and Carr (1996, p. 32) give us three basic reasons for this statement:

- "The standards set clear targets and expectations for students, teachers and parents.
- Students improve their ability to monitor and evaluate their own work and assess their progress as they work with standards-based sources of evidence.
- Products and performances provide an ongoing, cumulative data source for measuring progress over time, within and across units."

As teachers, we may agree or disagree with the whole idea of state-mandated tests based on standards, or we may like or not like the test itself. These preferences aside, success on these tests is vital given the extreme interest in accountability. "Strong standardized scores earn us the trust of our communities as we begin to demonstrate measurable progress on local criterion-referenced and alternative assessment" (Schmoker and Marzano, 1999, p.20).

> **Students need to see what acceptable levels of performance look like.**

How can record-keeping systems be organized to effectively keep track of student progress?

Grading and record keeping are often thought of as summative, end-of-the-line endeavors, rather than vital, living instructional tools. Standards-based education gives us cause to reconsider, even reinvent, what we do in this important area. The old notions and ways need to be reconsidered. "Most educators and non-educators assume that grades are precise indicators of what students know and can do in a subject area. Additionally, it is assumed that current grading practices are the result of careful study . . ." (Marzano and Kendall, 1996, p. 13). Marzano and Kendall then go on to tell us that grade reporting developed haphazardly and inconsistently and that it is extremely difficult to know what a particular grading scheme really indicates about a student's achievements.

> Grading and record keeping are often thought of as summative, end-of-the-line endeavors, rather than vital, living instructional tools.

It is necessary to find an alternative to traditional grade reporting to adequately keep records concerning the relative mastery of standard benchmarks.

Although A, B, C, D, and F may provide useful comparisons of student achievements within one organization, without a commonly accepted standardized grading system based on content, rather than numerical scores, grades will continue to prove to be a poor basis for interorganizational comparisons of student competence in a particular subject area.

It is necessary to find an alternative to traditional grade reporting to adequately keep records concerning the relative mastery of standard benchmarks. With each benchmark comes the need to assess a student's performance. Perhaps a viable way of indicating performance would be to divide them into advanced, proficient, basic, and novice levels. Suggested meanings for these four levels are described in the generic performance levels for both declarative and procedural benchmarks. Declarative benchmarks involve "knowing," and procedural benchmarks involve "doing."

General Scales for Declarative and Procedural Benchmarks

Generic Performance Level for Declarative Knowledge	Generic Performance Level for Procedural Knowledge
Advanced Performance: Demonstrates a thorough understanding and articulates complex relationships and distinctions	Carries out the major processes/skills inherent in the procedure with relative ease and automaticity
Proficient Performance: Demonstrates an understanding of the important information; is able to exemplify that information in some detail	Carries out the major processes/skills inherent in the procedure without significant errors, but not necessarily at an automatic level
Basic Performance: Demonstrates an incomplete understanding of the important information, but does not have severe misconceptions	Makes a number of errors when carrying out the processes and skills important to the procedure, but still accomplishes the basic purpose of the procedure
Novice Performance: Demonstrates an incomplete understanding of the important information along with severe misconceptions	Makes so many errors when carrying out the processes and skills important to the procedure that it fails to accomplish its purpose

From *Designing Standards-Based Districts, Schools, and Classrooms* by Marzana and Kendall, (1996, p. 217).

Students and parents need to understand the implications of advanced, proficient, basic, and novice performance. To use any new grading system requires educating all concerned.

The classroom teacher is the most appropriate educator to collect assessment data regarding student performance on standards and benchmarks (Marzano and Kendall, 1996). There are so many options open to classroom teachers: forced-choice items, essay questions, portfolios, teacher observations, student self-assessment, etc.

Some of these assessment methods can be graded objectively. Others require more subjective procedures that can be aided significantly by the use of rubrics. Rubrics are scoring guides that indicate the criteria on which a piece of student work will be evaluated. Rubrics give characteristics of each level of performance, from work that barely shows evidence of meeting a standard (novice) to work that satisfies the very basic qualifications (basic), to work that meets expectations (proficient), to work that exceeds expectations (advanced). Sometimes numbers are used to indicate quality in conjunction with descriptions or by themselves.

When you combine the switch to standards with the advent of a new grading system, communication is vital.

The important thing to know about rubrics, regardless of the words or numbers chosen to describe quality, is that they set clear expectations of what we are asking students to do to achieve mastery. Rubrics allow for detailed commentary on work because they refer students to established criteria. The "targets" become clear. There also are numerous books and parts of books dedicated to the topic of rubric writing and use.

Like content and performance standards, rubrics are not going away. They make sense. They are good for teachers and good for students.

Just as a new grading scheme requires educating both students and parents, this is also the case when we switch to standards-based education. When you combine the switch to standards with the advent of a new grading system, communication is vital. Frequent notes and letters home help calm the potential fears parents can have about any change. On the page that follows is a sample letter that accomplishes several goals at once:

- it informs parents about what is being studied
- it reiterates the importance and use of standards
- it shows the relative weighing of the standards

Attaching a sample rubric with a brief explanation would also be helpful.

Sample Letter to Parents

Dear Parents:

In this unit, we will be studying an important concept called percolation. To master this topic, students will have to know and be able to do a number of things. Specifically, each student will have to

Standard 1: Understand the basic characteristics of percolation.

Standard 2: Understand basic information about soil and different types of soil.

In addition, each student will have to show competence in a number of general skills and abilities. These include:

Standard 3: Effectively design a bar graph depicting the results of an experiment.

Standard 4: Effectively generate and test a hypothesis.

Standard 5: Contribute to the overall effectiveness of a group.

Standard 6: Make an effective oral presentation.

To calculate your student's letter grade for the unit, I will use the following scheme:

Standard 1: 25% of grade

Standard 2: 25% of grade

Standard 3: 10% of grade

Standard 4: 20% of grade

Standard 5: 10% of grade

Standard 6: 10% of grade

Unit activities will include readings from the science text, quizzes, homework assignments, a lab experiment and report, demonstrations, and group work. Your son's or daughter's performance in these activities will provide the information that will be used to make judgments about his or her performance on these six standards.

From *Designing Standards-based Districts, Schools and Classrooms* by Marzano and Kendall (1996), p. 213.

The use of standards makes the "grading process more concrete, up front, and honest," according to Zmuda and Tomaino (1999, p. 60). In their article, "A Contract for the High School Classroom," they report that students appreciate knowing the criteria for assignments as expressed in standards. They mark each assignment with the standard(s) it involves. Standards provide the glue that ties together the teacher's purpose of instruction, the materials needed to accomplish a task, and the student's understanding of expectations.

Now the quandary—how do we evaluate, record, and communicate student progress in a standards-based classroom? In chapter 7, it is recommended that districts provide a variety of approved grading and record-keeping alternatives from which a teacher may choose the best for his/her classroom. In the absence of district guidance, teachers can take the matter as a challenge and design their own system.

Susan Colby presents a common sense approach in her article "Grading in a Standards-Based System" printed in the March 1999 issue of *Educational Leadership*, p. 53. She approached the development in a four step process:

> **Standards provide the glue that ties together the teacher's purpose of instruction, the materials needed to accomplish a task, and the student's understanding of expectations.**

1. **Design a workable format.** Colby uses one page per student (possible because she teaches at the elementary level). On the left of each page is listed all the curriculum standards for each subject. Each page also contains a grid used for recording scores.

2. **Define codes to be used.** Colby uses **P** for performance assessment, **A** for assignment, **O** for observation, and **%** for percentage of correct answers. A plus sign is used to indicate proficiency, a check mark for in progress and a minus sign for no demonstration of proficiency. Colby chose to use a different color for each nine-week grading period. The time frame could be a week or a month or whatever makes sense. This code is necessary because some students will require more opportunities to become proficient in certain standards and marking the horizontal columns no longer makes sense because of varying student activities.

3. **Create an easy-to-access grade book.** Colby places the individual grade sheets in a three-ring binder. This binder is used all day long, not just to indicate test grades.

4. **Monitor and adjust the system.** One obvious adjustment that makes so much sense in terms of standards is that one assessment or assignment may show proficiency related to several different standards. Hence, there may be a number of marks made as the result of one student activity. This led Colby to mark each assessment and assignment with the standards to be demonstrated, just as Zmuda and Tomaino (1999) had done in their high school classrooms.

Extracts from a Standards-Based Grade Book—Grade Two

Name _____

+	Has demonstrated proficiency of Learner Outcomes

✔	In progress on Learner Outcomes

−	Has not demonstrated proficiency of Learner Outcomes at this time

P = performance assessment

A = assignment

O = observation

% = percentage correct/test

Science					
The Learner will: • compare and contrast related living things that procedure in similar ways					
• identify examples of plant reproduction (spores, seeds, cuttings, buds, shoots)	+O	+O	+O	✔O	
• know that related living things reproduce in similar ways	✔O	+A	+O		
• analyze the reasons for changes observed in plant growth (or lack of growth)					
• observe the changes in plant growth (or lack of growth)	✔O	✔O	53%		
• record plant growth	+A	+A			
• identify plant parts					
• know plant parts (for example, roots, stems, leaves, flowers)	✔O	✔O	77%		
• know the effect of gravity on roots and stems	✔O	✔O	88%		

From: Colby, S. A. (1999). Grading in a Standards-Based System *Educational Leadership* 56 (6) page 53.

One of the most significant advantages in using this system is the change in emphasis from what is taught to what is learned. It becomes clear which students are progressing in relation to each standard and which students need extra help and time. The classroom becomes very learner-centered as standards, assessments, assignments, and instruction are aligned. The teachers who use this system say it helps them to make conscientious decisions about assessments and assignments that would best fit the standard, the student, and the amount of time allocated.

Beyond grading individual students and monitoring the progress of each, the dilemma of keeping track of standards—when and in what depth they are emphasized and learned—brings us back to the need for a checklist. In every teacher's records there should be a chart listing all the standards/benchmarks that apply to their students. A math specialist for the fourth and fifth grade would need a list of the math standards for those students. A second-grade teacher in a self-contained classroom would need the standards for all the subjects in a second grade. A high school world history teacher would need the subject-specific standards. To the right of each standard should be a grid where dates and assignments and assessments can be listed that pertain to each standard. This kind of record-keeping is tedious—but necessary—to assure that teachers are aware of the standards and remain vigilant in their teaching.

One of the most significant advantages in using this system is the change in emphasis from what is taught to what is learned.

How can districts and states help local schools, teachers, and students meet the challenges of standards?

Set clear goals.

Every rung on the accountability ladder plays an important role in the climb toward standards mastery. States and districts must play roles that go beyond measurement and enforcement. They must guide and support local teacher efforts to achieve results that are significant and enduring. This support should be comprehensive and on-going. Below is a list of nine areas where states and districts can make a difference.

1. **Set clear goals.** Without clear vision, it is almost impossible to hit a target. The same is true with standards. If they cannot be seen and touched and grappled with, the changes of students

meeting and exceeding standards are slim. Vague, "beat-around-the-bush" content standards with nebulous, hard-to-identify performance standards will only serve to frustrate building-level staff who are charged with teaching and then assessing mastery.

2. **Provide clear distinction between content standards and performance standards and then assure that the two are in perfect alignment.** When this occurs, concern over "teaching to the test" will be nonexistent. Teaching to the test will parallel teaching to the standards.

3. **Provide explicit guidance concerning alignment of state standards and the curriculum teachers are accustomed to teaching.** Classroom teachers have a limited amount of time, and that time should be devoted to planning and implementing lessons, not doing paperwork. Alignment is a major task that should be accomplished by non-classroom personnel, perhaps in concert with teachers who have been given release time or paid time when school is not in session.

4. **Create and consistently apply a staff development plan that involves every facet of standards-based education.** This plan can be based on Bloom's Taxonomy. We need to make sure teachers have the tools they need to:

   - be knowledgeable of the content of standards documents, in-depth for their own subject area and/or grade level, and cursory in all the other areas.

   - comprehend/understand the meaning and intent of each and every standard they will teach.

   - analyze the standards to know how they compare and contrast and where they fit into lessons and units.

   - apply the standards to everything they expect their students to know and be able to create the learning environment necessary to facilitate the mastery of standards.

   - evaluate their own instructional and assessment strategies in light of the expectations embodied in the standards documents.

> **Standards are lasting. So, too, must be our efforts to help teachers be at their best in the classroom.**

This is a tall order. Standards are lasting. So, too, must be our efforts to help teachers be at their best in the classroom. Staff development needs to be in the least common denominator of teachers, that is, at grade-level meetings, team meetings, and departmental meetings within each school. These sessions must be interactive and purposeful. Districts and states provide personnel and plan for local staff development. They must insist that teachers gather to teach each other about what works in their classrooms.

5. **Carefully consider research-based innovations in student grouping and scheduling.** The whole point of having content and performance standards is to increase student learning. With that in mind, districts and states must examine classroom and school practices that prove to be promising in other areas. For instance, multi-year student-teacher assignments are showing great promise, as are multi-age classrooms. Block scheduling has been around in many forms for years, and yet many districts have ignored the positive results reported at elementary, middle, and high school levels. District personnel must avidly read professional journals such as *Educational Leadership, Kappan, Middle School Journal*, etc., to stay abreast of innovative practices that are improving student learning across the country.

Still, we know that all children can learn.

6. **Develop a fair and user-friendly system of reporting progress.** The previous section deals with classroom record-keeping systems. Teachers should not have to struggle with this issue. It is a paperwork problem and districts need to present options to be used on local levels that translate easily into the format needed by districts and states. How frustrating it can be for teachers to not have a convenient and concise way to keep track of what standards are met by which students and then have an even less efficient way of communicating progress to their district. We should not rely on yearly tests to paint the whole picture of the efficacy of our classrooms!

7. **Put into place a way of looking at improvement rather than bottom-line raw data.** Everyone involved in public education recognizes that school populations provide their own unique challenges. When it comes to academic achievement, some populations present a "readiness to learn" that exceeds others. It is no secret that poverty impoverishes more than the body in many cases. "As in most large districts, middle and high SES (socioeconomic status) groups consistently and significantly out-performed low SES groups." (Marzano and Kendall, 1996, p. 197).

Students from low income homes struggle academically for many reasons. Pick up journals, newspapers, and textbooks on any given day and the picture is painted for us. Still, we know that all children can learn and this fact must be supported by districts and states by giving deserved credit for improvement, not just raw scores on assessments. This carries over into the arena of comparisons. It is blatantly unfair to put schools side-by-side and compare achievement when the playing field is not level. Yes, we should have the same high expectations for all students; this is what standards are all about (Marzano and

Kendall, 1996). But the journey toward mastery does not need to be littered with unfair comparisons along the way.

8. **Provide time for standards-based education to work.** This is a huge undertaking. Merely writing, printing, and disseminating standards will not bring improvement in student learning. Standards are not fads. The last decade of the century, of the millennium, has been spent in the pursuit of standards for teaching and learning. Even the standards themselves are under, or should be under, continual scrutiny. Allowing time for their implementation in classrooms is vital. This does not mean waiting one or two years for improvement to occur, but five years or ten years. With any systematic charge there are growing pains and setbacks. We must allow for these and not throw out what could possibly be the most promising reform effort yet. As teachers, we often lament, "This, too, shall pass." Districts and states must work with determination to make sure that standards-based education does not fall victim to that lament!

9. **Put in place support systems to provide information and guidance to schools and teachers.** "You are not alone" should be the message heard loud and clear by building level staff. Continual dialogue opportunities must be provided in non-threatening and encouraging environments. Collegial support and team-like responsibility and accountability structures will foster professionalism that will pay positive dividends in terms of student learning!

With any systematic charge there are growing pains and setbacks.

How can the standards movement succeed?

Teachers must believe
that all students can
learn.

The success of any reform measure floats precariously in a crowded pool of variables. Because content and performance standards affect all aspects of public education, the hope that their development, implementation, and enforcement will benefit students certainly depends on a myriad of issues. The list that follows is a general sampling of the conditions that would contribute to, and nurture, the standards movement.

1. **Teachers must believe that all students can learn.** This condition touches the inner-most part of an educator's heart and philosophy. Notice that the statement does not end with "the same amount in the same time frame." We need a deep understanding and continuous curiosity about how students learn, linked to a full instructional toolbox from which to choose a variety of strategies. These two elements allow us to confidently state that all our students can learn. High expectations for all of our students is crucial. In *Standards for Our Schools,* Tucker and Codding (1998) state emphatically that " . . . the single most important obstacle to high student

achievement in the United States is our low expectations of students—not just students who are poor and come from minority backgrounds but . . . most of our students."

Tucker and Codding (1998) also adamantly believe that student effort is more important than natural ability as a determinant of achievement. The practice of tracking students by ability groups in early grades is vicious because most students find themselves "stuck," unable to make the transition to a supposedly higher-achieving group. This denies children the opportunity for a good education. Tucker and Codding contend that, "The best way for this country to reverse that course (low expectations, diminishing student effort) is to set a high standard that is the same everywhere and for everyone and make it clear to all but the severely handicapped that they are expected by all the adults in their lives to reach that standard. Period." In the March 1999 issue of *Educational Leadership*, we are told that requiring all students to be included in measures of educational assessment, regardless of the accommodations necessary for participation, is a key factor in ensuring high expectations for every student (Kearns, Kennedy, & Kleiner, 1999, p. 77).

> **Student effort is more important than natural ability as a determinant of achievement.**

2. **The alignment of prescribed standards to a district and/or school's curriculum is an essential condition for the success of standards-based education.** Unless a standards-based curriculum is made available when the standards for a state are first unveiled (a rare event), it will be up to those who must both teach the curriculum and make certain that the standards are included to look for overlapping and gaps. Hopefully, classroom teachers will not have the alignment task all to themselves. Most districts will need to appoint committees to oversee the task of alignment. The process does not have to take months. Grade-level and/or subject-area committees made up of people very familiar with both documents can accomplish the task. Even though the two may be close, there will certainly be areas covered in the curriculum with no apparent counterpart in the standard, and vice versa. These gaps need to be addressed. When content standards and the prescribed curriculum are parallel, teachers can be assured that the content is likely to be assessed. Both the performance benchmarks and the skill level requirements in math, science, and several other related subject areas have risen in the past 30 years with the growth of a technology-based job market. Often state and district curriculum have not kept pace. Changes in instructional strategies, especially the addition of new strategies, will probably be needed.

3. **Administrators need to be ardent supporters of standards and the implementation of standards-based education by their teachers.** Creating a standards-based school requires the principal to play a key role in supporting teachers as they establish standards-based classrooms. To do this effectively, Lockwood (1998, p. 27) urges greater levels of professional development for principals. They must not only be informed, but they should also be participants in standards development. "Administrators also are the link between community members, parents, and the schools, and they need to embrace standards-based teaching and testing in order for it to succeed as part of the school's or district's comprehensive effort to educate all children" (Lockwood, 1998, p. 7).

Tucker and Codding (1998) recount Phil Daro's assertion that " . . . the touchstone of a school focused on standards is a school focused on student work" (p. 125). They also ask us to imagine a school in which the principal's in-box is always full of student work, and that this work is the centerpiece of his or her meetings with teachers and departments. Imagine a principal who walks into classrooms and talks with students while carefully observing student work.

> Creating a standards-based school requires the principal to play a key role in supporting teachers as they establish standards-based classrooms.

This level of principal involvement is the thrust of "School Leaders Look at Student Work," an article in the March 1999 issue of *Educational Leadership*. The authors, Graham and Fahey, assert that, "Through a collaborative assessment process, school leaders work to identify what standards truly mean for teaching and learning" (p. 25). The process involves administrators coming together for what they call "7-Step Collaborative Assessment Conferences":

1. Read or observe the student work in silence.
2. Describe the work, suspending judgement.
3. Ask questions about the work, the child, and the assignment.
4. Speculate about what the student is working on.
5. Listen to the presenting teacher who reveals the content of the work.
6. Discuss implications for teaching and learning.
7. Reflect on the conference.

   Adapted from Seidel, et. al. (1997).

When administrators order the requirements within standards, when they are familiar with what mastery (as well as lack of it) looks like, and when their commitment keeps them involved every day with classrooms, then they will be supportive from a knowledgeable position.

4. **Staff development should be centered on understanding and implementing standards-based education.** Where on the priority list does funding for development fall? Sadly, usually toward the bottom of the list. Wise districts will recognize this before it is too late to benefit major reform efforts such as standards-based education (Lockwood, 1998, pp. 4–5). In many cases, "To teach to the new standards, teachers will also need to assume new competencies . . . they need an infusion of professional development that is standards based, practical, and constructivist. . . . Teachers need professional development that extends beyond exhortations to highly practical strategies that they can use in their classrooms with new content" (Lockwood, 1998).

The Pittsburgh Public Schools provide workshops like most districts, but with a "twist." In education, we know that seeing something done, experiencing a concept or skill, and hands-on opportunities lead to greater comprehension and more in-depth learning. In Pittsburgh, that is exactly what teachers are getting. In addition to workshops and in-service training, teachers are shown in-class demonstrations. These demonstrations provide structured support for weeks at a time. Demonstration teachers go into the classroom and work with individual teachers. They teach a class while the classroom teacher observes. Demonstration teachers are in no way serving in evaluative capacities, so when the demonstration teacher takes a seat in the classroom and watches the regular teacher teach using target instructional techniques, non-threatening feedback is given and the process repeats. The demonstration teacher does not document the teacher's performance.

Demonstration teachers go into the classroom and work with individual teachers.

Whatever the format, staff development aimed at more effective teaching and learning of standards should provide a balance leading to in-depth teacher understanding of the standards and concrete, strategy-laden methodology. Another element that must not be ignored is the assessment component of standards-based education. A common mistake made by states and districts involves "putting the cart before the horse," or assessing students on newly adopted standards before making every effort to provide effective staff development on standards-based instruction. The assessment component is pervasively important and should be a part of staff development that occurs before students are assessed. Teachers need to know what to expect in terms of assessment, both in content and format.

5. **In addition to a strong and consistent program of staff development, teachers need solid, standards-based material and texts.** One of the first questions teachers are

likely to ask of principals and district personnel is, "How does the material I currently use mesh with the standards I am now asked to use to organize my classroom practice?" (Lockwood, p. 7) Unless teachers are provided with time to align standards and material, they must rely on others to accomplish this alignment. Rarely are teachers given release time or paid time during vacations to take an in-depth look at the materials/standards correlation and do necessary planning. If a district or state could provide this opportunity, the benefits would outweigh those of having personnel other than classroom teachers take on the responsibility. Ideally, individuals closest to the student learning process should be charged with the task.

Once a determination is made concerning currently used materials, efforts should focus on obtaining additional materials, even the adoption of new texts. Publishers are producing texts and materials that are supposedly aligned to national standards developed by subject area organizations such as the National Council of Teachers of Mathematics and the National Council of Teachers of English. Decisions should not be made by one person, but by a committee comprised primarily of classroom teachers. As Lockwood (1998, p.7) urges, "Buyer beware." The array of computer technology available to enhance instructional programs is growing exponentially. Teachers and schools must use common sense and restraint when purchasing systems. Decisions should be based in large part on recommendations made by other school faculties that have personal experiences with software, etc., rather than relying on computer sales representatives or displays at conferences. Large sums of money and lengthy contracts with dealers can use up limited funds and yet not bring results in student performance improvement.

Decisions should not be made by one person, but by a committee comprised primarily of classroom teachers.

6. **Everyone within the school structure should be presented with an incentive program involving rewards and consequences based on measures of student improvement.** In an ideal world, we would all rely on the intrinsic reward of satisfaction derived from learning and achievement. Unfortunately, intrinsic rewards are often not enough to motivate most people when it comes to academics. While we should continue to emphasize and model the satisfying nature of learning and achievement, a realistic approach leads us to thoughtfully design extrinsic rewards, with subsequent external consequences.

The system of rewards and consequences should be motivational. For students, awarding certificates recognizing improved student performance towards standards mastery can be motivational as long as they are awarded for sustained, meaningful improvement and not subject to capricious distribution that invalidates the honor of receiving them. Commonly used motivational strategies such as picnics, "free" periods, field trips, and popcorn parties that teachers find effective can be used as rewards for student/class improvement and achievement.

A system of consequences is more difficult to develop, with inherent dangers including stunting a student's desire to work hard, discouragement to the point of immobilization, and the very real possibility of being unfair in terms of punishing students for possible circumstances outside their control, such as undiagnosed learning problems and psychological problems that block academic progress. Districts and states generally have consequences ranging from required after-school tutoring or summer school, to grade level retention. Receiving extra help is in no way a consequence, though the circumstance and time frame in which the assistance is given may lend a sense of punishment. These practices should be under continual scrutiny.

A system of consequences is more difficult to develop, with inherent dangers. . .

Tucker and Codding (1998, p. 239) recommend the development of an incentive system for school faculty and district employees that rewards improved student performance and provides consequences for lack of improvement. Once acceptable levels of performance are established, the following key elements are recommended:

- Engaging a highly qualified academic probation manager for each school.
- Requiring that the staffing plans, hiring, budget, and program plan of a school on academic probation be approved by the probation manager.
- Authorizing the probation manager to recommend the expedited dismissal of any member of the staff of a school on probation, subject to applicable laws and regulations.
- Requiring every school on academic probation to select an approved external technical assistance provider or school reform network with which to affiliate and to use the assistance provided by that organization or network.
- Authorizing the probation manager to recommend the reconstitution of any school on academic probation. Any staff member of a school on probation that has been recommended and approved for reconstitution would lose his or her job unless that staff member is offered another job in the district by another school.

Schools, districts and states should proceed with caution when dealing with reward/consequences decisions. These decisions should not be hasty, but rather very deliberate with a healthy dose of counsel from a variety of sources, not the least of which are those who are the targets of the rewards and consequences.

7. **Developing appropriate assessment measures that define progress toward student mastery of standards is a vital component of standards-based education.** Content standards came first. National organizations and states began by defining what students should know and be able to do. Perhaps the more complex task is the writing of performance standards. After all, coming up with curriculum—the "what" of education—is an age-old process. Content standards organize the curriculum. Knowing if students master the standards—in other words, finding evidence of mastery—is in many ways a more recent need within the school setting. From a practical point of view, what good are standards if we have no way of gauging if students know and are able to do what we expect?

Standards-based education deserves a chance to succeed.

8. **Because standards-based education is not a fad but rather an enduring reform measure** (Schmoker and Marzano, 1999), **adequate time must be given for content and performance standards to make a difference in student learning.** Anyone who has been involved in public education, or has merely observed educational practices over time, undoubtedly observes how the proverbial pendulum swings when it comes to reform efforts. Education "powers that be" are notorious for jumping from one program to the next without real understanding that meaningful change takes time—time to evolve, to fail, to learn from failure, to regroup, to improve, and, ultimately, to make a difference for students. Standards-based education deserves a chance to succeed. This means allowing for refinements as a result of experience, and then modifying implementation. It may take years for districts and states to see steady growth in student performance. The work and the wait will be worth it.

Thoughtful educators realize that this list of variables and conditions is incomplete. As schools, districts, and states navigate the challenging minefield of standards-based education implementation, the list will continue to grow and be personalized to suit local circumstances.

Exploring Subject Area Standards

National professional subject-area organizations have developed standards and grade level benchmarks that have been used by most states as they compiled their own distinct standards. Informed as they were by the national organizations, state standards documents vary widely in terms of rigor. A comparison was done between students' scores on state assessments and the same students' scores on the National Assessment of Educational Progress. It was found that many students scored very high on their states' assessment, and yet very low on NAEP (Tucker and Codding, 1998). The purpose of this book is not to assess individual state standards. That will be up to interested parties within the states. However, the next section in this book addresses the issue of "standards for standards."

The intent of this chapter is to give an overview of the standards, along with sample benchmarks, that have been developed by national organizations. These standards provide a look at general areas, most of which appear within state standards documents. Again, the rigor found within each area will vary from to state. We begin with a list of professional subject-area organizations.

National professional subject-area organizations have developed standards and grade level benchmarks that have been used by most states as they compiled their own distinct standards.

Professional Subject-Area Organizations

The Arts
Music Educators National Conference
1902 Association Drive
Reston, VA 22091
703-860-4000
http://www.menc.org/

Civics and Government
The Center for Civic Education
5146 Douglas Fir Road
Calabasas, CA 91203
818-591-9321
http://www.civiced.org/

Economics
The National Council on Economic
Education
1140 Avenue of the Americas
New York, NY 10036
212-730-7007
http://www.nationalcouncil.org/

Foreign Language
American Council on the Teaching of Foreign
Languages
Six Executive Plaza
Yonkers, NY 10801-6801
914-963-8830
http://www.actfl.org/

Geography
National Council for Geographic Education
1600 M Street, NW, Suite 2500
Washington, DC 20036
202-775-7832
http://multimedia2.freac.fsu.edu/ncge/

Health Education
Association for the Advancement of Health
Education
1900 Association Drive
Reston, VA 22091
703-476-3437
http://www.aahperd.org/cgi-bin/counter.pl/
aahe/aahe.html

History
National Center for History in the Schools
UCLA, 231 Noore Hall
Los Angeles, CA 90024
310-825-4702
http://www.sscnet.ucla.edu/nchs/

Language Arts
National Standards for the English Language
Arts Project
The International Reading Association,
Division of Research
800 Barksdale Road
P.O. Box 8139
Newark, DE 19714-8139
302-731-1600, ext. 226
http://www.reading.org/

Mathematics
National Council of Teachers of Mathematics
1906 Association Drive
Reston, VA 22091
703-620-9840
http://www.nctm.org/

Physical Education

National Association for Sport and Physical
Education

1900 Association Drive

Reston, VA 22091

703-476-3410

http://www.aahperd.org/cgibin/counter.pl/
naspe/naspe.html

Science

National Science Education Standards

2101 Constitution AVE., NW

HA 486

Washington, DC 20418

202-334-1399

http://www.nap.edu/readingroom/books/nses/

Social Studies

National Council for the Social Studies

3501 Newark St., NW

Washington, DC 20016

202-966-7840

http://www.ncss.org/

Technology Education

International Technology Education
Association

1914 Association Drive

Reston, VA 20191-1539

703-860-2100

http://www.iteawww.org/

Vocational Education

National Center for Research in Vocational
Education

University of California, Berkeley

2150 Shattuck Avenue, Suite 1250

Berkeley, CA 94704

510-642-4004

http://vocserve.berkeley.edu/

Now we will list some of the standards for Language Arts, Mathematics, Science, United States History, and The Arts. Other standards may be accessed using the Web addresses provided in the list of organizations. There is a wealth of information available. The detail to which individuals access and use the information will depend on interest and investment in particular subject areas and grade levels. Following each list of standards will be sample benchmarks labeled by level. Level I is for K–2, Level II is for grades 3–5, and Level III is for grades 6–8. These are provided to give a sense of how the mastery of one standard involves a methodical build-up of knowledge and skills. This again points to the importance of grade-level to grade-level articulation among teachers.

The Standards for Language Arts

The standards for writing:

1. Demonstrates competence in the general skills and strategies of the writing process.
2. Demonstrates competence in the stylistic and rhetorical aspects of writing.
3. Uses grammatical and mechanics conventions in written compositions.
4. Gathers and uses information for research purposes.

The standards for reading:

5. Demonstrates competence in the general skills and strategies of the reading process.
6. Demonstrates competence in general skills and strategies for reading a variety of literary texts.
7. Demonstrates competence in the general skills and strategies for reading a variety of information texts.

The standard for listening and speaking:

8. Demonstrates competence in speaking and listening as tools for learning.

Sample Benchmarks for Writing Standard 1:

- Demonstrates competence in the general skills and strategies of the writing process.

Level I (K–2) Benchmarks:

- Prewriting: discusses ideas with peers, draws pictures, writes key thoughts.
- Drafting and revising: uses strategies to draft and revise written work (begins to add descriptive words and details, deletes extraneous details, rereads, rearranges words and sentences to clarify meaning).

Level II (3–5) Benchmarks:

- Prewriting: uses graphic organizers, story maps, webs, brainstorms with groups.
- Drafting and revising: elaborates on central ideas, writes with attention to voice and audience, tone.

Level III (6–8) Benchmarks:

- Prewriting: outlines, uses published pieces as writing models, constructs critical standards.
- Drafting and revising: uses organizational schemes, uses sensory words, and checks for a consistent point of view and for transitions, constructs critical standards.

The Standards for Mathematics

1. Uses a variety of strategies in the problem-solving process.
2. Understands and applies basic and advanced properties of the concepts of numbers.
3. Uses basic and advanced procedures while performing the process of computation.
4. Understands and applies basic and advanced properties of the concepts of measurement.
5. Understands and applies basic and advanced properties of the concepts of geometry.
6. Understands and applies basic and advanced concepts of statistics and data analysis.
7. Understands and applies basic and advanced concepts of probability.
8. Understands and applies basic and advanced properties of functions and algebra.
9. Understands the general nature and uses of mathematics.

Sample Benchmarks for Mathematics Standard 1:

- Uses a variety of strategies in the problem-solving process.

Level I Benchmarks:

- Draws pictures to represent problems.
- Explains to others.
- Uses whole number models (blocks, tiles, or other manipulative materials) to represent problems.

Level II Benchmarks:

- Understands the basic language of logic in mathematical situations (and, or, not).
- Uses trial and error and the process of elimination to solve problems.
- Represents problems and situations in a variety of forms (e.g., translates from a diagram to a number or symbol).

Level III Benchmarks:

- Uses a variety of reasoning processes (e.g., reasoning from a counter example, using proportionality) to model and to solve problems.
- Understands how to break a complex problem into simpler parts or use a similar problem type to solve a problem.
- Understands that there is no one right way to solve mathematical problems but that different methods (e.g., working backwards from a solution, using a similar problem type, identifying a pattern, etc.) have different advantages and solutions.

The Standards for Science

Earth and space:

1. Understands basic features of the earth.
2. Understands basic earth processes.
3. Understands essential ideas about the composition and structure of the universe and the Earth's place in it.

Life sciences:

4. Knows about the diversity and unity that characterize life.
5. Understands the genetic basis for the transfer of biological characteristics from one generation to the next.
6. Knows the general structure and function of cells in organisms.
7. Understands how species depend on one another and on the environment for survival.

Physical sciences:

8. Understands basic concepts about the structure and properties of matter.
9. Understands energy types, sources, and conversions, and their relationship to heat and temperature.

Nature of science:

10. Understands the nature of scientific knowledge.
11. Understands the nature of scientific inquiry.
12. Understands the nature of enterprise.

Sample Benchmarks for Life Science Standard 4:

- Knows about the diversity and unity that characterize life.

Level I Benchmark:

- Knows that plants and animals have features that help them live in different environments.

Level II Benchmarks:

- Knows different ways in which living things can be grouped (e.g., plants and animals, pets/non pets, edible and non-edible plants).
- Knows that plants and animals progress through life cycles of birth, growth, development, reproduction, and death; the details of these life cycles are different for different organisms.

Level III Benchmarks:

- Knows that animals and plants have a great variety of body parts and internal structures that serve specific functions for survival (e.g., digestive structures in vertebrates, invertebrates, unicellular organisms, and plants).
- Knows ways in which living things can be classified

Standards for Historical Understanding

1. Understands and knows how to analyze chronological relationships and patterns.
2. Understands the historical perspective.

Standards for United States History

1. Understands the characteristics of societies in the Americas, Western Europe, and Western Africa that increasingly interacted after 1450.
2. Understands cultural and ecological interactions among previously unconnected people resulting from early European exploration and colonization.
3. Understands why the Americas attracted Europeans, why they brought enslaved Africans to their colonies and how Europeans struggled for control of North America and the Caribbean.
4. Understands how political, religious, and social institutions emerged in the English colonies.
5. Understands how the values and institutions of European economic life took root in the colonies, and how slavery reshaped European and African life in the Americas.
6. Understands the causes of the American Revolution, the ideas and interests involved in shaping the revolutionary movement, and the reasons for the American victory.
7. Understands the impact of the American Revolution on politics, economy, and society.
8. Understands the institutions and practices of government created during the Revolution and how these elements were revised between 1787 and 1815 to create the foundation of the American political system based on the U.S. Constitution and the Bill of Rights.
9. Understands the United States territorial expansion between 1801 and 1861 and how it affected relations with external powers and Native Americans.

Sample Benchmarks for Historical Understanding Standard 1:

- Understands and knows how to analyze chronological relationships and patterns.

Level I Benchmarks:

- Knows how to identify the beginning, middle, and end of historical stories, myths, and narratives.
- Knows how to develop picture timelines (of their own lives or their family history).
- Understands calendar time in days, weeks, and months.

Level II Benchmarks:

- Understands calendar time in years, decades, and centuries.
- Distinguishes between past, present, and future time.

Level III Benchmarks:

- Knows how to organize events of historical importance into broadly defined eras.
- Knows how to impose temporal structure on their historical narratives (e.g., working backward from some issue, problem, or event to explain its causes that arose from some beginning and developed through subsequent transformations over time).

The Standards for Geography

The World in Spatial Terms:

1. Understands the characteristics and uses of maps, globes, and other geographic tools and technologies.
2. Knows the location of places, geographic features, and patterns of the environment.
3. Understands the characteristics and uses of spatial organization of Earth's surface.

Places and Regions:

4. Understands the physical and human characteristics of place.
5. Understands the concept of regions.
6. Understands that culture and experience influence people's perceptions of places and regions.

Physical Systems:

7. Knows the physical processes that shape patterns on Earth's surface.
8. Understands the characteristics of ecosystems on Earth's surface.

Human Systems:

9. Understands the nature, distribution, and migration of human populations on Earth's surface.
10. Understands the nature and complexity of Earth's cultural mosaics.
11. Understands the patterns and networks of economic interdependence on Earth's surface.
12. Understands the patterns of human settlement and their causes.
13. Understands the forces of cooperation and conflict that shape the divisions of Earth's surface.

Environment and Society:

14. Understands how human actions modify the physical environment.
15. Understands how physical systems affect human systems.
16. Understands the changes that occur in the meaning, use, distribution, and importance of resources.

Uses of Geography:

17. Understands how geography is used to interpret the past.
18. Understands global development and environmental issues.

Sample Benchmarks for Places and Regions Standard 4:

- Understands the physical and human characteristics of place.

Level I Benchmarks:

- Knows the physical and human characteristics of the local community (e.g., the neighborhood, schools, parks, creeks, shopping areas, airports, museums, sports stadiums, hospitals, etc.).
- Knows that places can be defined in terms of their predominant human and physical characteristics (e.g., rural, urban, forest, desert; or by types of landform, vegetation, water bodies, climate).

Level II Benchmark:

- Knows how the characteristics of places are shaped by physical and human processes (e.g., the effects of agriculture on changing land use and vegetation; effect of settlement on the building of roads; relationships of population distribution to landform, climate, vegetation, or resources).

Level III Benchmarks:

- Knows the human characteristics of places (e.g., cultural characteristics such as religion, language, politics, technology, family structure, gender, population, land uses, and levels of development).
- Knows the causes and effects of changes in a place over time (e.g., physical changes such as forest cover, water distribution, temperature fluctuations; human changes such as urban growth, the clearing of forests, development of transportation systems).

The Standards for The Arts

Art connections:

  1. Understands connections among the various art forms and other disciplines.

Dance:

  2. Identifies and demonstrates movement elements and skills in performing dance.

  3. Understands choreographic principles, processes, and structures.

  4. Understands dance as a way to create and communicate meaning.

  5. Applies critical and creative thinking skills in dance.

  6. Understands dance in various cultures and historical periods.

  7. Understands connections between dance and healthful living.

Music:

  8. Sings, alone and with others, a varied repertoire of music.

  9. Performs on instruments, alone and with others, a varied repertoire of music.

10. Improvises melodies, variations, and accompaniments.

11. Composes and arranges music within specific guidelines.

12. Reads and notates music.

13. Knows and applies appropriate criteria to music and music performances.

14. Understands the relationship between music and history and culture.

Theater:

15. Demonstrates competence in writing scripts.

16. Uses acting skills.

17. Designs and produces informal and formal productions.

18. Directs scenes and productions.

19. Understands how informal and formal theater, film, television, and electronic media productions create and communicate meaning.

20. Understands the context in which theater, film, television, and electronic media are performed today as well as in the past.

Visual Arts:

21. Understands and applies media, techniques, and processes related to the arts.

22. Knows how to use the structures (e.g., sensory qualities, organizational principles, expressive features and functions of art.)

23. Knows a range of subject matter, symbols, and potential ideas in the visual arts.

24. Understands the visual art in relation to history and cultures.

25. Understands the characteristics and merits of one's own artwork and that of others.

Sample Benchmarks for Music Standard 13:

- Knows and applies appropriate criteria to music and music performances.

Level I Benchmarks:

- Knows personal preferences for specific musical work and styles.
- Responds through purposeful movement (swaying, skipping, dramatic play) to selected prominent characteristics or specific music events (meter changes).

Level II Benchmarks:

- Knows music of various styles representing diverse cultures.
- Knows appropriate terminology used to explain music, music notation, music instruments and voices, and music performances.
- Identifies the sounds of a variety of instruments.

Level III Benchmarks:

- Identifies specific music events (entry of an oboe, change of meter, return of refrain) when listening to music.
- Understands how the elements of music are used in various genres and cultures.

Sample Benchmarks for Theater Standard 15:

- Demonstrates competence in writing scripts.

Level I Benchmarks:

- Improvises dialogue to tell stories.
- Selects interrelated characters, environment, and situations for simple dramatizations.

Level III Benchmarks:

- Refines and records dialogue and action.
- Creates improvisations and scripted scenes based on personal experience, imagination, literature, or history.

Sample Benchmarks for Visual Arts Standard 21:

- Understands and applies media, techniques, and processes related to the arts.

No Level I Benchmarks

Level II Benchmarks:

- Knows the differences between art materials (paint, clay, wood, videotape), techniques (shading, varying size or color, overlapping), and process (casting, constructing in making jewelry, subtraction in sculpture).
- Uses art materials and tools in a safe and responsible manner.
- Knows how different media, techniques, and processes are used to communicate ideas, experiences, and stories.

Level III Benchmarks:

- Understands what makes different art media, techniques, and processes effective or ineffective in communicating various ideas.
- Knows how the qualities and characteristics of art media, techniques, and processes can be used to enhance communication of experiences and ideas.

Setting Standards for Standards

So we have content standards in 49 of our 50 states, with Iowa being the only state not to have state-adopted standards. While the state standards documents share common elements, they still "vary greatly in how they are organized, in the level of detail and specificity of their content prescriptions, and in the clarity of their expression" (Archibald, 1998 p. 2). It is vital that several processes be in place to serve in watchdog capacities. The advent of mandated state standards is recent and, no matter how admirable, needs to be continually scrutinized.

The major organizations to first examine state content standards are the American Federation of Teachers (AFT), the Council for Basic Education (CBE), and the Fordham Foundation. The AFT was the first. Their latest report, published in 1997, was entitled "Making Standards Matter." The CBE study, published in 1998, focused on mathematics and English language arts. The Fordham Foundation, in 1998, published reviews of mathematics, science, history, and geography, having focused on English language arts in 1997.

State standards have tremendous influence over teaching and learning. They have made their way into almost every public school in America. Organizations such as AFT, CBE, and Fordham are fulfilling a critically important service. Currently, there is no model or "best practice" for writing and implementing standards. Nor is there agreement on the criteria to use for judging the quality of standards. Most teachers will probably accept the standards given to them by state authorities, but there will inevitably be others who will question the quality of the standards that affect what happens in their classrooms. If you are one of those teachers with the inclination to examine standards, this chapter provides a variety of measures currently in use. If you are not so inclined due to time constraints or a general acceptance that the development process of standards is a trustworthy one, this chapter will still help you be a smarter consumer of standards-based education.

The Fordham Foundation assesses subject area content standards in different ways. Following is a summary of the general areas scrutinized in various subject area. (Fordham Report, 2(5), July 1998 pp. 30–36).

> **State standards have tremendous influence over teaching and learning.**

English Language Arts/Reading Standards

- Purpose, audience, expectation, assumptions
- Organization of standards
- Disciplinary coverage of standards
- Anti-Literacy or Anti-Academic Requirements or Expectations: negative criteria

History Standards

- Clarity: How well are the standards written?
- Organizations: How well are the standards organized and linked to state assessment?
- Historical soundness: What is the nature and quality of history found in the standards?
- Historical content: Are specific studies of United States, European, and World History found in the standards?
- Absence of manipulation: Do standards avoid manipulation, bias, indoctrination, and/or inappropriate applications of history?

Mathematics Standards

- Clarity: The success the document has in achieving its own purpose.
- Content: Is the state asking K–12 instruction in mathematics to contain the right things, and in the right amount and pacing?
- Mathematical reasoning: Do the standards as a whole and throughout demand attention to the structural organization by which the parts of mathematics are connected to each other?
- Negative qualities: The presence of unfortunate features of the document that injure its intent or alienate the reader to no good purpose or, if taken seriously, will tend to cause that reader to deviate from what otherwise good, clear advice the document contains.

Science Standards

- Purpose, expectation, and audience
- Organization
- Coverage and Content
- Quality: unambiguous, flexible, covers basics, demanding
- Negatives: not accepted as scientific, pseudoscientific, or scientifically discredited constructs; implications of science bias

The analyses conducted by the Fordham Foundation reveals that most states failed to set clear and rigorous expectations for what children should know and be able to do. Six questions resulted from the Fordham investigation:

1. Why are many state standards so vague?
2. Why are many state standards hostile to knowledge? (slanted in favor of skills)
3. Why are many states standards entranced by "relevance"?
4. Why do many state standards confuse classroom means with educational ends?
6. To what extent did national standards impact state standards?

The Council for Basic Education (CBE) focused on the rigor of state standards. The two key components are as follows:

1. essential concepts and skills
2. sophisticated learning

The American Federation of Teachers (AFT) rated states content standards on the degree to which they compiled with a "common core curriculum." The AFT reviewers used the following five criteria (Archibald, 1998):

1. Reference to grade levels or clusters of grades.
2. Detailed and comprehensive.
3. Firmly rooted in the content of the subject area.
4. Clear and explicit.
5. Course-based standards must specify which courses are required of all students.

The results of the reviews by AFT, CBE, and Fordham vary widely. This brings into questions the reliability of any of the measures. Perhaps they should be considered formative rather than summative in nature.

The National Education Goals Report of 1996 (p. 11) reports that Colorado took a somewhat brave path as state officials enlisted the assistance of Colorado citizens to help judge the quality of its standards. Over 3,000 citizens and groups were asked to rate the standards on a scale of 1–5 using five key questions. Those asked to participate included parent organizations, teachers, superintendents, public libraries, school boards, university presidents, and the general public.

The National Education Goals Panel has developed ten criteria for effective standards.

The questions were as follows:

1. Is the content standard a statement of what a student should know and be able to do?
2. Is the content standard specific and clear?
3. Is the content standard meaningful for today's world?
4. Is the content standard inclusive (that is, something every child can learn)?
5. Is the content standard a worthy goal for student learning?

The National Education Goals Panel has developed ten criteria for effective standards:

1. World-class: at least as challenging as current standards in other leading industrial countries, though not necessarily the same.
2. Important and focused: parsimonious while including those elements that represent the most important knowledge and skills within a discipline.
3. Useful: developing what is needed for citizenship, employment, and life-long learning.
4. Reflective of broad consensus-building: resulting from an iterative process of comment, feedback, and revision including educators and the lay public.
5. Balanced: between the competing requirements for:
   • depth and breadth;
   • being definite/specific and being flexible/adaptable;
   • theory or principles and facts or information;
   • formal knowledge and applications;
   • being forward-looking and traditional.
6. Accurate and sound: reflecting the best scholarship within the

discipline.

7. Clear and usable: sufficiently clear so that parents, teachers, and students can understand what the standards mean and what the standards require of them.

8. Assessable: sufficiently specific so their attainment can be measured in terms meaningfulness to teachers, students, parents, test makers and users, the public, and others.

9. Adaptable: permitting flexibility in implementation needed for local control, state and regional variation, and differing individual interests and cultural traditions.

10. Developmentally appropriate: challenging but, with sustained effort, attainable by all students at elementary, middle, and high school levels.

> Source: Goals 3 and 4 Technical Planning Group on the Review of Education Standards (1993). *Promises to keep: Creating high standards for American students* (Publication 94-01), pages iii–iv. Washington, D.C., National Education Goals Panel.

In their book *Standards for Our Schools*, Tucker and Codding (1998, pp. 43–45) provide yet another list of what standards should be:

1. Standards should be used to set a very high foundation requirement for all students; reflecting high expectations for everyone.

2. Standards should be useable by students, in the sense that a student should be able to look at the standards and know instantly what topics have to be mastered, what knowledge has to be gained, and what kind of work he or she has to produce to meet the standards.

3. Standards should be experienced in a way that enables them to be used to motivate students to take tough courses and to study hard.

4. Standards should actually require that students know the things that lie at the heart of the core subjects in the curriculum, but knowledge by itself is not enough. Both the standards and the assessments that go with them should mirror the requirements of life outside the school as much as possible.

5. Standards, to be successful, must have broad support among teachers and the general public.

6. Standards should be competitive, in the sense that they should be at least as high as the standards to which students

Both the standards and the assessments that go with them should mirror the requirements of life outside the school as much as possible.

... states have the
monumental task of
making hard decisions
about what we expect
our students to know
and be able to do.

in other countries are held in the same subjects as the same
grade or age levels.

7. Last, standards should be as universal as possible.

How can we identify standards that are clear, purposeful, organized,
balanced between knowledge and skills, comprehensive, yet reasonable to accomplish within our school-bound time constraints? What a
daunting question! It illustrates the need for consistent, continual vig-
ilance on the part of everyone involved. Given the broad, over-
whelming nature of the possibilities for standards presented to us by
the subject area organizations, states have the monumental task of
making hard decisions about what we expect our students to know and
be able to do. Clearly, some voluntary federal guidelines would help
the states gain balance and perspective in their efforts.

Concerns and Cautions

As with any change or reform attempt, the advent of standards-based education brings with it a list of concerns. Often, concerns arise because of unavailability of information or because answers to questions simply are not known when they are posed. Here is a partial list of concerns presented without answers or responses. Some may be legitimate, others may not. But the very act of asking questions and voicing concerns can lead to improvements, because we are forced to consider issues.

1. As of 1995, all states are required to submit their standards and assessments to the federal government for approval. This was brought about by the linkage of *Goals 2000* to the *Elementary and Secondary Education Act*, which allocates billions of dollars to the nation's schools. It is feared that "federal regulation may extend much more directly into what is taught, how it is taught, the conditions in which it is taught, and how it is tested" (Ravitch, 1995, p. 19).

2. How do we know the standards we are using are the best ones for students? Arriving at a core of content is politically contentious, complicated, and laborious (Lockwood, 1998).

3. Some state standards documents contain much more content than could ever reasonably be taught in 180 seven-hour days. The principle of "less or more"—translated as "students learn more when we teach less, but teach it well"—is grossly violated in many standards documents (Schmoker and Marzano, 1999, p. 19).

4. Poor-performing schools may react in counterproductive ways to standards and subsequent assessment and accountability. They may work to implement them or they could dismiss them. "They also might look at where they are and where they need to be. When they see this chasm, they could end up completely paralyzed" (Lockwood, 1998, p. 39).

5. Teacher training and retraining is needed to insure instruction appropriate for many standards. Until teachers are comfortable with their own skills and insight, we should not hold children responsible for mastery of the standards.

6. All schools and student populations are not created equal. This lack of equity covers facilities, resources, personnel, parental involvement, community commitment and support, and the readiness to learn of the pupils who attend. It is not fair to test all students on the same standards if there is no equity of educational opportunity (Ravitch, 1995, p. 163).

7. Critics caution that "adequate provisions may not be made in either standards or assessments matched to the standards for nontraditional student populations." They go on to question if the standards and assessments " assume a certain previous educational experience and college-bound aspirations." (Lockwood, 1998)

8. Accountability based on standards may become too high-stakes, with consequences imposed that have the potential to bankrupt public schools of teachers and administrators. Threats of retribution rarely have long-term positive effects, especially when it comes to education.

9. Having uniform standards for a state may restrict creativity and hinder growth of interdisciplinary instruction. Because standards are subject specific, they may further segment the larger body of content and prevent connections.

10. The standards movement may narrow curriculum. Teachers will hesitate to spend time on topics and issues that are not explicitly addressed in standards documents because of time constraints and the knowledge that there will not be assessment attached to such topics.

11. Mastering or not mastering standards will sort students and allow for widespread tracking. Standards and their assessment may create winners and losers.

Teacher training and retraining is needed to insure instruction appropriate for many standards.

12. Standards-based education sounds a lot like outcome-based education (OBE) to some. Both OBE and standards identify what students should know and be able to do. They both work backwards " to construct a curriculum that will achieve the appropriate outcomes." (Ravitch, 1995) Just because standards have not entered the realm of moral or character development like OBE, they may cross the line once they have achieved widespread acceptance in the states.

13. Standards-based education may be considered just another fad, another way for educators to justify their existence. Reforms like this come around every decade or so. Schools attempt to change how they do business, and by the time they feel on the verge of making a positive difference for children, time is called and a new game begins.

14. Some critics say that standards are for English speaking, middle class students. What about our growing population of non-English speakers? How will bilingual and English as a Second Language (ESL) programs fall under standards-based curriculum?

Continual scrutiny is good and healthy. It is how we grow.

This is by no means a complete list of the concerns and cautions associated with standards-based education. Everyone involved with the public education has concerns that may or may not have been touched on here. The point must be made that questioning an endeavor does not necessarily mean that it is not worthwhile. Continual scrutiny is good and healthy. It is how we grow.

Conclusion

Standards set our sights on outcomes, on where we are heading in terms of student learning.

The very nature of standards emphasize what is learned more than what is taught. Standards set our sights on outcomes, on where we are heading in terms of student learning. In this sense, they make schooling learner centered. "When used as guidelines to curriculum and teaching, standards offer a promising tool for improving achievement for all students" (Wheelock, 1996, p. 3).

Now that most states have learning/curriculum standards and are working towards developing assessments to measure when and if we meet them, can we sit back and let them, as if by magic, reform public education? The answer is a resounding *no*. All the standards in the world will not cause learning to happen. They provide the target; the myriad of other variables are the arrows. Taking the arrows from the quiver, placing them in the bow, aiming, and then having enough strength to shoot them takes energy, know-how, and commitment. To make a lasting difference, we need teachers who are committed to high expectations for student achievement, resources that speak explicitly to what those expectations are, and skills to motivate, instruct, and hold accountable the students in their classrooms.

Lynn Olson (1999, p. 1) tells us that standards are a very American idea. They say to us, "Take responsibility for our actions. Focus on results." The death of many, if not most, education reform movements results from a lack of patience, consistency, and continuity, the jumping from one emphasis to another. Content and performance standards are basic. They do not resemble fads. Built into the whole notion of standards is the goal of quality learning outcomes for all students. How can that go away?

Questions still remain. That is actually a good sign. If we stop questioning, we stop growing. As the information age continues, as we learn more and more about the learning process, as we experience societal shifts, and as our priorities change, so will standards-based education continue to evolve. . . . What about our growing need for English as a Second Language (ESL)? How will ESL affect the standards movement? Will competition arising from high stakes accountability drive us too hard? Will the debate involving classic knowledge and high tech "know how" present too many disagreements on what should be learned/assessed? Will the political climate allow for national standards and will they supplant state standards?

> Questions still remain. That is actually a good sign. If we stop questioning, we stop growing.

We have our work cut out for us! It is fine to take a break and celebrate the widespread acceptance of the concept of standards-based education. Then we must roll up our sleeves, respond to questions, and then ask some more. "However visionary they may be, standards by themselves cannot work the magic of school reform. They only set the stage for both harder and smarter work among professionals who want to improve teaching and learning" (Wheelock, 1996, p. 3).

References

Archibald, D. A. (1998). The reviews of state content standards in English, Language Arts, and Mathematics: A summary and review of the methods and findings and implications for future standards development. Paper commissioned by the National Educational Goals Panel.

Colby, S. A. (1999). Grading in a standards-based system. Education Leadership, 56(6), pp. 52-55.

Finn, C. E., Petrilli, M. J., & Vanourek, G. (1998). The state of standards. Thomas Forham Foundation Report, 2(5).

French, D. States Role in Shaping a Progressive Vison of Public Education. Phi Delta Kappan, 80(3), pp. 184ff.

Graham, B. I. & Fahey, K. (1999). School leaders look at student work. Educational Leadership, 56(6), pp. 25–27.

Gunter, M.A., Estes, J. H., & Schwab, J. (1999). Instruction: A Models Approach. Needham Heights, MA: Allyn and Bacon.

Harris, D. E. & Carr, J. F. (1996). How to use standards in the classroom. Alexandria, VA: Association for Supervision and Curriculum Development.

Kearns, J. F., Kleinert, H. L., & Kennedy, S. (1999). We need not exclude anyone. Educational Leadership, 56(6), pp. 33–38.

Lockwood, A.T. (1998). Standards for Policy to Practice. Corwin Press, Inc. Thousand Oaks, CA

Marzano, R. J. & Kendall, J. S. (1996). Designing Standards-based Districts, Schools, and Classrooms. Association for Supervision and Curriculum Development, Alexandria, VA & McREL. Aurora, CO

McREL. http://www.mcrel.org/

National Commision on Excellence in Education, "A Nation at Risk: The Imperative for Educational Reform" Washington: 1983, p.5.

Olson, L. (1999). Shining a spotlight on results: Quality counts '99. Education Week on the Internet.

O'Neil, J. (1999). Core knowledge and standards: A conversation with E. D. Hirsch, Jr. Educational Leadership, 56(6), pp. 28–31.

Ravitch, D. (1995). National standards in American education: A citizen's guide. Washington, D.C.: The Brookings Institute.

Scherer, M. (1999). Perspectives. Educational Leadership, 56(6), p. 5.

Schmoker, M. & Marzano, R. J. (1999). Realizing the promise of standards-based education. Educational Leadership, 56(6), pp. 17–21.

Sills-Briegel, T., Fisk, C., & Dunlop, V. (1996-97). Graduation by exhibition. Educational Leadership, 54(4).

Tucker, M. S. & Codding, J. B. (1998). Standards for our schools. San Francisco, CA: Jossey-Bass Publishers.

Wheelock, A. (1996). Mathematics and science standards: What do they offer the middle grades? The Harvard Education Letter, XII (5).

Willis, S. (1997) National standards: Where do they stand? Education Update, 39(2). Alexandria, VA: Associaton for Supervision and Curriculum Development.

Zmuda, A. & Tomaino, M. (1999). A contract for the high school classroom. Educational Leadership, 56(6), pp. 59–61.